MW01223941

THE BOOK OF SERVICE

THE BOOK OF SERVICE

Thaylor Iron Rope

Cover Book art by Joe McHugh

REDEMPTION
PRESS

© 2014 by Thaylor Iron Rope. All rights reserved.

Published by Redemption Press, PO Box 427, Enumclaw, WA 98022
Toll Free (844) 2REDEEM (273-3336)

Redemption Press is honored to present this title in partnership with the author. The views expressed or implied in this work are those of the author. Redemption Press provides our imprint seal representing design excellence, creative content and high quality production.

No part of this publication may be reproduced, stored in a retrieval system, or transmitted in any way by any means—electronic, mechanical, photocopy, recording, or otherwise—without the prior permission of the copyright holder, except as provided by USA copyright law.

All Scripture quotations, unless otherwise indicated, are taken from the New King James Version. Copyright © 1982 by Thomas Nelson, Inc. Used by permission. All rights reserved.

Scripture quotations marked KJV are taken from the King James Version of the Bible.

Scripture quotations marked (NLT)are taken from the Holy Bible, New Living Translation, copyright ©1996. Used by permission of Tyndale House Publishers, Inc., Wheaton, Illinois 60189 USA. All rights reserved.

Scripture quotations marked (NIV) are taken from the Holy Bible, New InternationalVersion®.NIV®. Copyright © 1973, 1978, 1984 by International Bible Society. Used by permission of Zondervan. All rights reserved.

ISBN 13: 978-1-63232-784-0
Library of Congress Catalog Card Number: 2014948606

Dedication

I am very thankful that God inspired me with thoughts and stories to grow upon. There are many people who have left a lasting impression and influence on me along the way of this journey.

I am thankful to my family and friends who encouraged me to write, preach, and teach. My appreciation to *Ray Martinez,* the former mayor of Fort Collins, Colorado, for helping me publish this book with his guidance, writing skills, and vast experience of publishing twelve books of his own. Ray certainly has inspired me to grow in the Word and has given me confidence to move forward with no regrets.

My grandmother, *Barbara Chapman*, led me to the Lord after I asked her how to become "born again." She was my lifesaver; and to this day, Grandma always prays for me as I do for her as well. My Grandma may look weak in appearance, but she is strong in spirit.

Joe McHugh, my high school art teacher, has always been a great encourager for me and lives a life of godliness that I want to emulate. I learned from his personal walk with Jesus. His Christian artwork of illustrations of Bible stories is a portrait of his character. Mr. McHugh was the first person who talked to me about Christ when I was in high school, and for that I am forever grateful.

The late *Nick Seaman*, my high school math teacher, who shared my burden of having a speech impediment. He always taught me that when I talk and stutter, "people can wait."

Pastor *Brent Cunningham*, associate pastor at Timberline Church, for often meeting with me for lunch or coffee to teach me about life and God's walk. I consider him a man of wisdom. Brent baptized me at Timberline Church on February 12, 2012 at 10:00 A.M.

Dick Foth, associate pastor at Timberline Church, for meeting with me and for encouragement with the ministry that God blessed me with. He and I have a lot in common.

Johnny Square, senior pastor of Iasis Church, for his willingness to hear from the common people and his personal guidance in my life and the lives of others.

Rick Richter, pastor at Iasis Church, for taking the time to listen to people on an individual basis. He has a genuine heart for God and his people.

To my *Anonymous Donor* for his generous financial support in the publication of this book. This donor felt led by God to support this ministry.

My mother, *Robyn Chapman*, who always "told it like it is." I remember when I was little and used to cry for my dad, Mom would always tell me, "Jesus is your real Dad." I am thankful for my mom for raising me to be a man and to respect myself.

God-Inspired Memorable Quotes

These are some memorable quotes that God inspired or impressed me with. They are examples of how God left a permanent imprint on my life to guide me and to help others along the journey of teaching the Word of God.

We are saved, but not safe.
You see Jesus' glory, but you don't know His story.
Live for God and not for your fears.
I thought maybe it is better to be created by Christ then to be related to Him.
If I live for myself I die with dishonor,
but if I live for Christ I die with honor.
I die not for earthly men but for the heavenly Man.
God created faith and man made religion.
The world's ways bring destruction, but God's ways bring reconstruction to build a new foundation in our lives.
Church is not always on Sundays but everyday,
because we are the church.
Don't bring the world into church;
bring the church into the world.
I am only the partaker, not the glory.
When I preach then I teach the people.
Lord, may I never depart from You,
but always be apart of You.
There is only one way to heaven and a lot of ways to hell!
People have to experience their own brokenness
before they can be healed.

You shouldn't let your environment influence you, but you should
be the one who influences your environment.
As a man proposes to his wife,
Christ proposed to us on the cross.
God wants us to be the people that we need to be,
not the people that we want to be.

People are willing to open up their bodies together
and to contract sexually transmitted diseases,
but are not willing to open up their hearts about Jesus.
God tests us so He can perfect himself in us.
I ask people where they are going in life and they have thought-out
answers. But when I ask them where
they will go in the afterlife, they are clueless.
Just as you came to God through the law,
you come to God through Christ.
If doctors can revive people who died,
so can God by raising Christ Jesus from the dead.
The Son of Man shows us how to live and
how to die for God.
People can wear a cross around their
necks or have tattoos, but the cross is in our hearts.
Women and men are like the animal that deceived them. (Authored
by my cousin Tony Castillo)
Christ is our missing piece who brings peace into our hearts.
I know what I am to this world, which is nothing,
but I am something to Christ.
Our prayers should be for change, not for fame.
Love brings truth while harshness brings evil.
Everybody wants to talk about Jesus,
but nobody wants to be like Jesus.
If we look at human love we see that it is selfish;
godly love is selfless.

CONTENTS

PREFACE

I have taken the time to present you with my personal journal entries and voyage with Christ. I call this book *The Book of Service* because it really captures my labor for Christ in bad times and in good times. I am committed to God's service and His direction in my life. People cannot better express themselves than attaching a pen to his or her thoughts. Paul, one of my favorite disciples, who I like to reference, expressed his thoughts and inspirations from God through the power of writing. His writings, as well as the other gospel writers, are continuously studied and pondered.

Because the Holy Spirit inspired the disciples' writings, the Scriptures seem to personalize our lives. What may give direction to me in one phase of my life, may give completely different insights to another person. The important discernment for all of us is to follow God's direction, not someone else's opinion. The inspiration of Scripture is godly, supernatural, and divine. I like what Ron Rhodes wrote about inspiration in his book, *What Does the Bible Say About …?.* In chapter one he states, "Inspiration doesn't mean the Bible writers just felt enthusiastic, like the composer of the "Star-Spangled Banner." Nor does it mean the writings are necessarily inspiring to read, like an uplifting poem. The biblical Greek word for inspiration literally means, 'God breathed. 'Because Scripture is breathed out by God—because it originates from Him—it is true and inerrant." The inspired word is incapable of mistakes.

Some of my journal entries are from my distresses or contentment in how I was treated or how others were regarded with contempt, love, empathy, and even hatred. Many of us have difficulties in life or abilities that differ from the majority of people. In my case, I have wrestled with a speech impediment for many years, much like Moses talked about when he was conversing with God, mentioning that he was "slow of speech." "And Moses said unto the LORD, O my Lord, I am not eloquent, neither heretofore, nor since thou hast spoken unto thy servant: but I am slow of speech, and of a slow tongue" (Ex. 4:10 KJV).

The blessing of being "slow of speech" is that when I am preaching and teaching, it seems to diminish or it is less noticable. I count this as a blessing from God's power through Jesus Christ who sent us his Comforter to help us know what to say at the right time, and also give us the strength to deliver the message. I like what Paul said, "for when I am weak, then am I strong" (2 Cor. 12:10 KJV).

Many of the chapters are compilations of my daily journal entries that I made over the last couple of years. I subsequently joined those daily entries into categories that are applicable to the chapters. During your read, you will see some specific journal entries by date. Also, for the sake of privacy for some people, various names in the stories were changed.

A Special Note from Ray Martinez

Thaylor Iron Rope and I met at a Timberline Church men's retreat a few years ago, and I knew from the moment we talked that God was impressing me to help him along his journey. Little did I know one of his journeys was to publish this book of God-inspired reflection.

During our initial conversation, I listened to Thaylor struggle through our conversation because of a speech impediment as he told me how he felt called into the ministry to serve God. My immediate reference was the story about Moses and how he was slow to speak. In my estimation, this man is another Moses in the making.

I have never seen a young person like Thaylor who is so deep-rooted by studying the Word daily. He is a Native American who is not a cultural warrior, but he is a tremendous prayer warrior. Time after time, I have witnessed his prayers come to fruition, undoubtedly the hand of God at work in his life. Thaylor makes a daily list of people to pray for. I make sure I'm on his list as well.

There is not any doubt in my mind that his studies, Bible courses through a university to become a minister, will make it become a reality for his service in the future. When you read this book, you will discover his ministry has already started. It's nothing for him to meet people at the right moment and place that touches their hearts and when they need prayer the most. He also ministers to other youth about the teachings of Jesus.

Because of his eagerness to document his God-inspired thoughts and prepare them for this publication, Thaylor typed the entire book into his smartphone. Later he transposed it into a laptop word processor document for the final manuscript submission. That's a lot of "thumb-typing." This book publication was a labor of love to help share the message of Jesus Christ. We are very thankful for God's encouragement and inspiration. Editing and piecing together this book has been one of the most pleasurable occurrences for me as I've helped Thaylor put together his book for publication.

CHAPTER 1

THE TRUTH OF THE MATTER IS

The Lord Christ Jesus came into the world to be crucified and resurrected from the dead. Also, to show us and leave us with an example of the Great Commission! We are to make disciples of all nations, baptizing people in the name of the Father, the Son, and the Holy Spirit. Christ is the Cornerstone of our faith and nothing else. But there are people who want to preach a new gospel, one that misleads God's people from Jesus. There are so many false doctrines that mislead people from God by trying to preach something that's not true about Jesus. There are those who say that Jesus never existed or that there is no proof of Him being real. I say these people are lost and have not surrendered their lives to God, for that is how you know who the real Christ Jesus is.

Jesus is real. For, if He isn't real, He wouldn't offend anyone. The one they are offended by is Jesus, who is God come in the flesh. Even today Christ offends people. It hurts and angers me because these so called "teachers" teach things that they do not understand.

> Now the purpose of the commandment is love from a pure heart, from a good conscience, and from sincere faith, from which some, having strayed, have turned aside to idle talk, desiring to be teachers of the law, understanding neither what they say nor the things which they affirm.
>
> (1 Tim. 1:5-7)

Those who do not teach the fundamentals of the trinity— God the Father, God the Son, and God the Holy Spirit, which are the teachings people need to learn about Christ Jesus and how He is the King of kings and Lord of lords—these teachers have strayed. They have gone off track by preaching this new gospel that has no substance to it and is not ordained by God.

Even some Christian denominations can lead people away from God as well. It is not the teaching of Christ that misleads individuals, rather the teaching of some teachers and pastors. It seems that some pastors preach their denominational doctrine first before the gospel of Christ. They are no better then the Roman soldiers who divided the garments of Christ while He was on the cross, for they do the same with the Word of God.

We, who are teachers or preachers, need to understand that the Bible is God's inspired Word for us to proclaim that Jesus is the Christ to all people. We are also to listen to the Spirit of God who comes from His Word. We, as children of God, need to study the Bible.

> For whatever things were written before were written for our learning, that we through the patience and comfort of the Scriptures might have hope.
>
> (Rom. 15:4)

Whoever preaches any other gospel besides the one that we have received, let him be held accountable.

> But even if we, or an angel from heaven, preach any other gospel to you than what we have preached to you, let him be accursed. As we have said before, so now I say again, if anyone preaches any other gospel to you than what you have received, let him be accursed.
>
> (Gal. 1:8-9)

We who are really laborers for the gospel of Christ are condemned to death because we die daily denying ourselves for His will, not ours. For you see the world knows these false teachers, but they do not know us, for they did not know Christ. And if I am hated, despised, and an outcast to the world, then let it be so. For I know Christ has called me to be a minister to the people of God. He is grooming me for this very purpose—to feed His flock and labor for Him and Him alone. Even though I wrestle with my flesh every day, I will always serve Christ Jesus.

I'm not wise, nor strong by myself, and I am slow of speech and tongue, but God has called me to minister to people of this world. When I preach the message that Christ has given me, I do not stutter, but speak with boldness. Jesus Christ is my foundation that brings salvation. To the people of this age I say this, you who think you are wise, are you really wise? And those of you who think you are strong, are you really strong? For if you were, you would repent of your sins and come to know Christ. But since you do not, this so-called wisdom and strength will work against you, and you may believe the false teachings you hear.

Jesus is the Son of the living God who came in the likeness of man to die for our sins. Christ is the anti-type of Adam, the first man who came from the dust of the earth. Christ came from the trinity of God. Even though I struggle and wrestle with my flesh about Christ coming into the flesh, I know my conversion was not in vain for I have changed from the inside out by the Spirit of Christ. That is how I know Christ came in the flesh. Faith is supreme above all human acts. I will always preach about Christ being crucified and resurrected from the dead. The Son of Man has come for you and me. May God bless all of you who rest in Him and those who will soon believe in Him!

Thank You, Jesus. You are the One who saved me and delivered me into the ministry. For that I thank you God! I will always share and spread the Word of God. I love You and I know You love me.

CHAPTER 2

IS IT ABOUT YOU OR ABOUT PASTORING

Many times we are confused if a pastor is representing his own best interests or representing God's interests to his people. Don't get me wrong; I'm not here to slam pastors. There are many great pastors who are serving Christ to the fullest extent in their roles, and as a labor of love. But, I have to share a couple of experiences that sadden me, but have also taught me how to always be sensitive to the spiritual needs of people.

In the beginning of my experience, my days started out good. On one occasion after a church service, the youth pastor told me, "Man when will we hang out? I miss hanging out." While I was talking to him, other people interfered with our conversation. Afterwards, I was still trying to talk with him. Because of his interest in others, the youth pastor continued to ignore me without replying. I felt like that youth pastor only liked the title of being a youth pastor. He didn't live up to what his position is supposed to be. Popularity was more important to him than building relationships.

I don't need a title like youth pastor to feel better about myself or to gain popularity. It hurts me to see a person with a sense of entitlement associated with his position. Instead of serving, it felt like he was preserving status for himself. My motto in this case is: "For I can do all things through Christ, because He is in all things of my life."

In another incident, I got into an argument with my mother, which was my fault. I did confess my error to Mom with an apology. God knows my heart, because we talked about it. You might say we had a heart-to-heart conversation. I asked the youth pastor to pray for me about the disagreement with my mom. His response was appalling and shocked me. What hurt me the most was his statement about my mom. He said that my mom's walk with Christ was "fake." The youth pastor spoke with boldness and it was hurtful. I know these kinds of statements had offended other youth members as well.

When the youth pastor finished praying with me, it made me sick, because this man doesn't even know my mother to make such a statement. That prayer was rendered useless. True, I am not a church member, but I certainly can see right through him. I feel sad and angry about this youth pastor, but I also know his true personality will be revealed to others. I'm certainly not a perfect man, but a broken person as well. It is Christ that will mold me into the man I need to be.

My lesson is to not mimic this kind of behavior, but rather teach people on the street. Christ needs people in the battle zone or on the front lines of serving His purposes. From my experience, this youth pastor is not leading these people. His messages are losing their impact and almost sound like rambling. However, that's done and over with. Regardless, we are all apart of the body of Christ. I certainly don't hold a grudge. I am unquestionably forgiving of any hurts caused by the youth pastor. We are all growing daily and have a lot to learn. Our prayers should be for change not for fame.

When I searched the Scriptures, the Bible has some classic examples of people struggling with egos and worldly friendship. Trying to please each other shouldn't interfere with our spiritual walks, so we must strive continuously. Here are some examples:

Jesus was explicit that not everyone who says "Lord, Lord, have we not done your works and many wonders?" will enter the gates of heaven. In fact, Matthew 7:23 says his answer to them will be, "I never knew you."

Another story in Acts 19:13-16, involved the seven sons of Sceva, a Jewish chief priest, who claimed to have the power and authority of Jesus. The seven sons tried to cast out demons. The whole show backfired on them when the demons answered and said they knew Jesus and Paul, but the demons didn't know them. Consequently, the demons attacked the seven sons of Sceva. This example illustrates that leadership in God's church requires genuine service.

Finally, Paul called Peter on the carpet when he started playing favorites with the crowd he associated with. Before James came with his crowd of people, Peter didn't hesitate to eat with the Gentiles. Upon James' arrival, Peter "withdrew and separated himself, fearing those who were of the circumcision" and what they may think of him. Peter's behavior even swayed Barnabas to be "carried away with their hypocrisy" (Gal. 2:11-13).

Journal Entry: Sunday, March 17, 2013

Yesterday was a good day and also today was a good start as well. People want to hear God's voice, yet they do not know how to listen. Christ showed me that His Word is His voice and that we should repeat and recite the Word of God. This is another way we can hear His voice. As Christians we are called to imitate Him because He is our foundation of salvation. I preach to myself at work, home, and wherever I go. I preach to not only myself but to God and the angels. I know there are people who want to hear God's voice. His voice is His Word from the Holy Bible, Christ's spoken words of salvation.

CHAPTER 3

NOT TO LOSE HEART

Distresses and suffering are always in the Christian life and we are to rejoice in them, knowing these tribulations are just for a split moment in our lives. Doubts come and go in our faith. I know I have doubted Christ before, but I have confessed that to Him and always will when I doubt, for I am forgiven when I repent of my sins.

I have a cross to bear and I will be steadfast in the faith, trusting Christ and going where the Word needs to be taken. I want to be a drink offering to those who are weak and need strength, so I, who am strong, can be made weak for them. I will confess that I doubted God and His Word not being real yesterday, but I know that it was the Devil tempting me and trying to deceive me.

The truth is we all doubt God, it doesn't matter who you are. I have learned not to focus on my doubts, but to focus on the faith God has given me in Christ Jesus, and also the gift of ministry He has ordained me with. As Jesus said: "If anyone desires to come after Me, let him deny himself, and take up his cross daily, and follow Me" (Luke 9:23). I like it when Christ says "deny yourself." It means deny your doubts, worries, and fears.

For example, the prophets from the Old Testament were men who took heed to God's law and His commandments. They were inspired by God to write the prophetic word and proclaim the message that was given to them. Now, of course, there was fear, anxiety, and distress, and they were even killed by their own countrymen. But, the prophets did not lose heart in their ministries. These men were hopeless just like we were. But now, God has showed us His purpose through His Son. The prophets didn't know their writings were going to be apart of the Bible. They just wrote the prophetic words that God divinely inspired them with to preach, express, and to proclaim!

I am a sinner and a wretched man who deserves hell, punishment, and judgment. The only hope that can save us all from hell is Christ Jesus. For I was born into sin and molded by despair, but when I stepped into God's light, I saw who I truly was in that darkness; and I knew that I couldn't go back into darkness.

> For the flesh lusts against the Spirit, and the Spirit against the flesh; and these are contrary to one another, so that you do not do the things that you wish.
>
> (Gal. 5:17)

We must be strong in our hardships, leaning on God and His Word because that's all you and I have to know that God truly exists.

By faith we understand that the worlds were framed by the word of God, so that the things which are seen were not made of things which are visible.

(Heb. 11:3)

We know that an ordinary person cannot instruct others without an instructor or a teacher, if you will. The Word of God came to those who were despised and looked down upon by the world. By faith they spoke what they heard and wrote down what they were told by God.

I had trouble having faith in this and thought, *how could God inspire the prophets to write down what He told them?* What happens if they forget some things or thoughts from God? But God has no limitations. That's what I was doing, putting limits on my Savior and not having faith in what He did through the prophets and apostles.

This past week I was tormented and swallowed by my thoughts, yet I prayed and preached to myself at night, so I did not lose heart. I felt the heat of the Devil. But when you're in hell and high water, it does not matter how you feel. You've got to keep on praising Christ Jesus and know that where there is suffering, there is also glory.

Yea, though I walk through the valley of the shadow of death, I will fear no evil; for You are with me; Your rod and Your staff, they comfort me, You prepare a table before me in the presence of my enemies; You anoint my head with oil; My cup runs over. Surely goodness and mercy shall follow me all the days of my life; and I will dwell in the house of the LORD Forever.

(Ps. 23:4-6)

In some point in our walk with Christ we will have to walk into the valley of the shadow of death, and it may not be comfortable. However, in these pressing times we learn more about God and ourselves. The world will know that we will die on our feet serving Christ rather than living in the world on our knees.

May God bless you and keep you in His mighty hands. God will never leave us nor forsake no matter what we are going through.

Thank You, Jesus. You are the strength to my spirit, soul, and mind. Keep me strong in Your name. You have started a work in me and I know You keep on working in me until You come back. I love You Jesus!

The following are a couple of journal entries I completed that express my feelings during my times of reflection and learning:

Journal Entry, Wednesday, Jan 9, 2013

Today, I found a problem that I was having with doubting Jesus and placing Him in a box. In times like this, I know that I shouldn't compartmentalize God, knowing that God's ways are not my ways; I am just a man and weak minded at times. I have prayed and asked for forgiveness, and that I will think with my spirit and not my mind. Now I know that the key is to have faith and believe in Jesus Christ alone. I need to get up out of this doubt and have confidence in my King! I have to think and live by God's Spirit, and not my human mind. For my mind is weak and foolish; I despise my sinful nature. I shall fast for my King and think and listen with my spirit in conjunction with God's Spirit, for His voice is small and truthful!

I thank You, my Jesus, for having mercy, love, and forgiveness on me!

Jan 9, 2013 (later in the day)

I am convinced that God told Dad to text me last night. I asked him how you say Jesus in Lakota (my Native American tribe language). "Wanikiya" means Jesus Christ. It came to me that my people knew God, but they called Him "Tunkasila," which means, "Father of many." Also, they didn't have any scripture references, but they believed and had faith in the Creator. What God revealed to me is that Wanikiya is my Chief over all chiefs. God gets close to us by using our culture, which is how we can understand more about God. There is a reason why He puts our souls and spirits in different cultural bodies, so that we may reach all of God's people. I am happy my Father showed me this because it makes me appreciate my culture and where my people came from. Also, He revealed to me how I need to preach and teach the gospel to my people on the reservations.

I thank my Chief for showing me these wonderful things of my culture. I thank you, Jesus, for showing me revelations that you are the Son of God!

Friday January 11, 2013

Today is a good day. I learned that Jesus had the same emotions and experienced some of the same things as us. It's interesting how that is. Jesus is the Son of God, yet He knows the struggles that we go through. In the past, people and myself, have tried putting Him in a box or limiting Jesus. The reason why Jesus did the miracles and healings was so we can have faith in Him. There are times in my life when I wished I had been raised in a church so that I would be much further in my walk with Jesus. However, we all have different stories that make us the people that we are.

These past two weeks, I have struggled with my thoughts and fears that lie in my mind. The reason why I am fasting tomorrow is to get away from my mind and move into God's Spirit. I have to pray and read the Word of God and not question things of God but live it.

I love you Jesus. Have mercy and forgive me; it is by your blood that I am saved!

Look at me, I am flesh and bones to you people and I am identified through my spirit by the Almighty. I fear Him more than men, demons, and the Devil. I want to rest with my Creator and see His wonders and live for His purpose and be with Him. My spirit cries out, how long Lord do I have to wait until You come back and take me away? I am weak minded and I just want to rest with my King for He is my strength! But I know I have to live for Jesus and only for Him, and not myself, for there is nothing good in me. It is the Spirit of Jesus who is in me: His way, His truth, His life! When I cry, it is the Holy Spirit who cries out to the Father.

I love You Jesus. Restore me in You.

Saturday, January 12, 2013

Praise be to Jesus Christ my Father, my Shepherd, my King! Tonight at Timberline Church, the head pastor, Dary, prayed for me. Before the service, Dick Foth saw me and hugged me and said, "You're cold." I explained to him that I rode my bike to church. In response, he said, "Thank you for your faithfulness." Ray, another friend and brother in Christ, said Dr. Foth's statement was a way of God speaking to me. I find it to be true, now that I am reflecting. After service I walked up to the front for prayer and I said to the lady who was with the prayer team, "Pray what's on your heart for me and I will pray for you." And she put oil on my hands and prayed for me, and in return, I prayed for the woman and her husband. And they said, "Thank you, we needed that." I said, "You're welcome."

The message was good; it was about what we need to know. The teaching was reviewing 2 Timothy 4:1-8, which was good and made me feel glad that I am a Christian. True, it is hard at times but I would rather be here than anywhere else.

Thank You, Jesus, for standing by me when no one else would. You restore my mind, soul, and heart, and for that I thank You.

Sunday, January 13, 2013

Today is starting out good; I am just trying to keep it together and not let my mind get the best of me. I wonder sometimes why my mind is so weak and I have doubts and unbelief in Jesus. I know that He is true and real; it's just my mind that is my weakness.

What's wrong with me God? Please show me Your ways and how to overcome my thoughts, doubts, unbelief, and fears. I'm so small and broken. Just take me away, crush me into pieces and rebuild me Lord, because I need you. Lord, please guide me through this darkness that is in my mind. I trust You and love You! Thank You, Jesus, for Your Spirit, love, mercy, forgiveness, peace, and joy! Please take me out of this darkness, Lord Almighty!

The Lord will cut you down; He knows where your footsteps are on the ground. There is nothing religious about Jesus because He spent time with the common people. Jesus healed and listened to the poor and needy.

Wednesday, February 27, 2013

Here I am reading 2 Corinthians 4:16:

> Therefore we do not lose heart. Even though our outward man is perishing, yet the inward man is being renewed day by day.

Even though my body is filled with flesh and bones, which is dying every second, every minute, every hour, every day, every month, and every year, I will still live forever because I rest in Christ. I live for Him, not for myself anymore.

The people of this world do not know God because they do not believe in Christ. For the wisdom of God is Christ, as it is written in 1Corinthians 1:30-31:

> But of Him you are in Christ Jesus, who became for us wisdom from God—and righteousness and sanctification and redemption—that, as it is written, "He who glories, let him glory in the Lord."

Last night I went to Mom's house and it was good to preach to them and show Mom and Nick scriptures. I like to teach them the teachings of Christ. I have a special burden for my cousin who lives with Mom because he just returned from the Marines and he has not been the same. Tony listens to the media and opinions that come from men. He says he is a Christian, which he is, but my cousin puts himself in a cage. He doesn't realize he has the keys to unlock himself. I pray for him and I love him, but he is in the Lord's hands now.

I know that am here for a reason, and it was for me to be a teacher and preacher for my Lord Christ Jesus. Even though the roads that I face are dark, it is for the will of God that I go through them.

Thank you, for you are my King, my Lord and you are my Father. Be with me Jesus forevermore! Amen.

CHAPTER 4

REVELATIONS FROM GOD

Today was a good day. I was talking with Ray about why I was struggling and he said we are often taken through tests. He said because I bounced back so fast, it was an indication to him that I was going through a test from God. He also said one reason why God tests us is to get us ready for the next turn of events. I think that's true. I am glad that Jesus tests us because we become stronger and closer to Him. As it says in Hebrews 12:11-13:

> Now no chastening seems to be joyful for the present, but painful; nevertheless, afterward it yields the peaceable fruit of righteousness to those who have been trained by it. Therefore strengthen the hands which hang down, and the feeble knees, and make straight paths for your feet, so that what is lame may not be dislocated, but rather be healed.

These are good verses that teach us a lot about the testing of God. When we are tested it means Jesus loves us and tests us to see how far we will go to reach Him. *Thank You, Jesus, for loving me first and showing me your beauty in your Word. I love You, Jesus!*

There are two things that I focus on: the gifts God has given me, and the anointing He has placed on me. I know that God can take my anointing away if I am not living the life He wants me to live. The key is to live by the Word of God because our actions speak louder than words. The gifts will never be taken away, but the anointing will if a person doesn't live the life Christ lived, meaning doing the will of our Father.

Christians are being deceived by the world and by some pastors. The reason is the pastors' words are empty, without any action in their lives that demonstrates Christianity. God is a good God. It is man who misleads people, not God. That is why it is important for Christians to read the Word on their own time and not to wait for the pastor to feed them. God gave us a free will, so the question is: will people do the will of their heavenly Father or do their own will?

I am an old-school Christian, meaning that I read the Scriptures, pray, talk about Jesus to people, and work at living the life of a Christian. People may know Hebrew and Greek words that are used in the Bible, but the life we live matters more to God the Father, God the Son, and God the Holy Spirit! God gave us faith and I shall use it.

Thank You, Jesus, for calling me to be your servant, your child, and your son. I thank You for blessing me all these years, even before I became a Christian and for the years to come.

Journal Entry, Tuesday, January 29, 2013

God inspired me to write this:

America the God-fearing country we once knew. America how you have turned away from God and into the hands of foolish men who do not have the fear of God in them. America, were you once filled with the wisdom of God? America how long will you listen to men's voices? When will you start to listen to the Almighty's voice who speaks love, truth, and authority to the old and the young? America, how come you have turned away from the Creator's hands that are full of light, righteousness, love, mercy, and forgiveness? America has turned to the hands of the wicked, and she is being devoured slowly, but surely, by unclean minds, unclean hearts, and unclean men. America is being assaulted by the riches of this world. America don't you know that you were birthed out of God, not men? Listen to the voice within you, for it is God. America, all I have to say is, you can do what you want, but as for my family and me, we will serve the Lord.

The world makes me laugh, the world says that to be a man you must dress a certain way and act in a particular manner. The world says that people should have sex with as many as they can and live life to the fullest. The world makes me laugh because they think they are so wise, and at the same time they are displaying how uneducated they are. The men and women of this world think they are rich, beautiful, and that nothing can touch them.

The world is dead wrong about these things, and Christ is alive.

Men and women are little children inside, being led by a wolf in sheep's clothing. I feel for these people, they are self-righteous, proud, and lusting after the world filled with vanity and filth. We as people are nothing and are broken inside and out. The world perceives people as obedient, but God sees them as disobedient. People should know that God gave His Son Jesus to the world to die for mankind.

We shall all do the will of God, as it says in Romans 6:18-19:

> And having been set free from sin, you became slaves of righteousness. I speak in human terms because of the weakness of your flesh. For just as you presented your members as slaves of uncleanness, and of lawlessness leading to more lawlessness, so now present your members as slaves of righteousness for holiness.

These verses are not intended to hurt people but to correct us, so the world will know that Jesus is King of heaven and earth.

Thank you, Jesus, for your love and how You loved us first. I hope I am doing You justice and making You proud. Be with me Lord, so I may be in your kingdom with You forever!

Monday, March 18, 2013

This weekend was breath of new, fresh air. God spoke wonders to me and I loved it! I heard thoughts that were not my own but His and I was renewed. I heard His voice clear as day and I know it was God because He spoke from His own words, from the Word of God.

Christians today say, "I want to hear from God," or "Where is God?" God gave us the Word, which is Christ. We as children of the Almighty God need to read the Bible. God gave us His Word because His Word renews us. In John 14:6, Christ said, "I am the way, the truth, and the life." This is why it is important to read Christ's words. They bring life to our spirits. I thank God for His Word because I don't know where I would be without the Bible.

CHAPTER 5

WHAT IS A CHRISTIAN

What is a Christian? We are the seeds of Christ and our jobs are to plant seeds, to be the light of this world, and most importantly to imitate Christ. I come across some Christians who try to find new teachings and new ways to live the Christian life. Some use the opinions of Christian authors and other people on how to live this life, which can be good to an extent. But if we, as Christians, don't take heed to God's instructions in His Word, then we are doing something wrong. As it says in 1 Thessalonians 5:21, we should "test all things and hold fast to what is good."

This means that we, as the offspring of Christ, should exam all things that men say with the Word of God. The scriptures are true, full of beauty and light. If we are Christians then we are dead to the world, but alive in Christ. I would rather die today and go to heaven then live to a hundred and go to hell. I shall live for my King who laid His life down for a wretch like me.

Today, we see not all, but some people, calling themselves Christians, when in fact they do not realize what they are saying. They call themselves Christians but do not conduct themselves as children of God. This is no surprise to God nor should it be to us. It is untaught people saying things they do not understand.

I once asked a man of the Catholic faith, "Would you minister to people about Christ Jesus?"

"No, I would not," he said.

There are other people like him who will not defend or proclaim Jesus. Where is their faith and conviction? Head knowledge is not enough and wearing jewelry and the "fine apparel" of a cross is not sufficient. If we have faith in Christ Jesus and no works of laboring for God, than our faith is dead (James 2:26). People misinterpret the scriptural mentions of "works" in the book of James. The works are not for us, rather they are for the Lord.

Some Christians can *talk the talk* but *they cannot walk the talk*. If you want to be an active Christian, then read the Bible, pray for people, talk to them about Jesus and what He has done in your life and what He can do for theirs. True faith rests in these kinds of actions, and the children of God are shepherded, and we imitate Him in our daily walk.

> If anyone among you thinks he is religious, and does not bridle his tongue but deceives his own heart, this one's religion is useless. Pure and undefiled religion before God and the Father is this: to visit orphans and widows in their trouble, and to keep oneself unspotted from the world.
>
> (James 1:26-27)

The way to over come trials and tribulations is by having faith with works. That is how we can tell that our faith is genuine and true to Christ Jesus. It may be spiritual or physical work that is needed, but with faith comes service to everyone. For we are all in need and that is what the body of Christ is for.

I come to all of you in love and peace in Jesus' name for that is who I bare witness for. We must all have faith in Christ and not in ourselves, or anything else; that is where our service and labor counts. The world tries to build for themselves riches, fame, glory and whatever else falls into those worldly categories. However, the question is: Can they take these worldly achievements to the grave with them? The world's works stem from selfish ambitions, which at the core root is sin.

Faith with works may not show how rich, or famous we are to the world. Our works branch from the Lord Christ Jesus. Jesus said: "For even the Son of Man did not come to be served, but to serve, and to give His life a ransom for many" (Mark 10:45). God's Servant came to the world to demonstrate faith and to serve the true and living God. I want everybody to know that our works are for the kingdom of God. The love that we have abounds in the Father and the Father in us. God wants everybody to grow in his or her faith, love, and hope in Him. We must be willing to serve so we can grow in the name of Christ Jesus. For if we draw closer to God, then He will draw closer to us and we will grow in wisdom, knowledge, insight, and understanding. May the Lord God of creation bless those who have faith and seek Him and who pray in His name. Christ Jesus loves you all. If we serve Him, we shall reign with Him.

Father, you have blessed me so much and I will always give you all the glory. I love you and I know you love me. Lord Jesus, I pray that my faith, trust, reverence, devotion, assurance, and intimacy are always in you alone. I will pray for the children of God and those who will soon believe in the Son of God. Amen.

Friday, January 25, 2013

Today is a good day because I finished the book of Psalm, which is the longest book in the Bible. Also last night I was pondering on death, and how people are scared of it. But if we rest in Christ, then our death glorifies God. Christ took the sting of death away when He hung on the cross for us.

It is also interesting to see that people are accepting man-made religions over Christ who is the Head over everything. Christ said, "I Am the Way, the Truth, and the Life" (John 14:6). The reason why people make these man-made religions is because they cannot handle the truth and what the Almighty brings to the table. Usually these people are unhappy because they feel like there is something missing. They are being brainwashed by the world. I feel bad for this generation because they are losing their freedom spiritually, physically, and mentally. There is one thing I have to say and it is: God created faith, man-made religion. And as I speak not on my own authority, but for The One who died for me, these are the words He gave me. Walking the Christ-like life is easier than man's religion.

Friday, February 16, 2013

A friend told me, "You're the only man your mom has in her life." I said, "It's not me, but it's Christ. Christ is the one who transformed me from a boy into a man. I am thankful for His strength, light, and Spirit that's in me. I love Christ because no one else knows who I truly am; the only one who knows is Christ. For Jesus is in my heart and He leads me by His Spirit. My boldness of speech and actions come from my King, not me, for I am only the partaker and He is the glory.

Thank You Jesus, for calling me into your light. Show me your ways and help me not be me, but more like You.

Friday, Feb 23, 2013

What do people live for in the world nowadays? They live for vanity, self-pleasure, fame, and the list goes on. What do I live for? I live for Christ and not myself. I am selfless toward myself, knowing that I am born into sin; the whole world is. However, Christ, the Son of God, died for the world. He became the curse for us, and for that I live for Him. For if I live for myself, I die with dishonor, but if I live for Christ, I die with honor. I deny myself for there is evil in me; and I battle myself everyday. But I am glad I have Christ to lean on and not myself. As I live, I live not for man's opinions, but for God's instructions, which come from His Word. I die not for earthly men but for the heavenly Man, Jesus Christ. And I say, *thank You.*

Sunday, Feb 24, 2013

God gave me a thought: *would I rather hear a message or give a message?* Meaning would I rather hear a message on Christ or give a message to a person about Christ? I remember I had to work on a Sunday morning a few weeks back and the people I attended church with asked why I wasn't there. I told them I had to work the morning shift, but they kind of made a big deal out of it. The point is this: it's better to give rather then to receive, just like Christ. My absence from church because of work allowed me to "give" and share the Word with others at work. That doesn't mean I couldn't learn more at church, but I am certainly grounded enough to share the Word and give back the Word to others and still grow. Jesus gave His life for mankind so we should imitate Him.

Thank You God for being a Father to me and for teaching me your ways.

Monday, Feb 25, 2013

Today I was at the gym with this kid, Scott, who is also a Native American. While I was talking to him about Jesus, I noticed that it was stuck in his mind that Native Americans are the best, and that's that! I talked with him about how Christ came to die for us, and how Christ was before the Native American ways or culture ever started. Scott claimed that when he was nine years old that he read the bible twice, and stated that Jesus had sex with His mom. I asked him where does it say that in the Bible and he said, "I don't know, but it does!"

It is interesting how Christ makes people scared and mad when they are confronted with the truth. That in itself shows that Jesus Christ is real—because His truth causes people to get upset. The reality is that Christ is "the way, the truth, and the life" (John 14:6).

This also made me annoyed because Native American people are being lied to by men's opinions. People should not believe in the hype, only the truth. When I heard this young person say these false things about Christ, I felt like a demon was saying those false words. What is even more shocking is that he claimed to be a Christian. If he truly is, he wouldn't fall away by saying such profane statements. What is important now is to pray for this boy and let my King do what He does best, save souls. I am hurt to see a kid like that make such false statements, but all we can do is pray for him.

Sunday, March 10, 2013

I have been a Christian for a year now, and in that time I have learned a lot about Christ and myself. There are times when I question God on some things and I question myself as well. Nevertheless, I can't turn my back on God because His name was written on my heart before I became a Christian.

There are times when doubts and unbelief come up in our walk with Christ. The key is to preach and teach about Christ, not only to yourself, but to others as well. Even when these doubtful times come up, we as the body of Christ need to pray to the head, which is Christ. He is faithful and will help us in troubled times. As Christians we can't worry about ourselves but let's be concerned for others. We must be selfless towards ourselves and use the gifts that God gave us for others. It is hard to be a Christian, but at the same time I am glad I found my Father who has made a man out of me. I will go through the same path as my Jesus did for He is within and with me! So I encourage you who read this to love the Lord with all your heart, soul, mind, and strength!

People have said to me, "Thaylor, you're such a nice guy." I always say, "Thank you and I thank God." Because the truth is, it is Christ and not me. I always have to deny myself because I died on the cross with Christ when I accepted Him in my life. It is the cross of Christ I boast about, not myself for being good. Alone, I am not good, because we as humans are born into sin. Alone, I have evil motives. But since I have accepted Christ in my life, I live, yet not I but Christ Jesus lives inside of me. Galatians 2:20 says:

> I have been crucified with Christ; it is no longer I who live, but Christ lives in me; and the life which I now live in the flesh I live by faith in the Son of God, who loved me and gave Himself for me.

I am glad that Christ lives in me because I have everlasting peace flowing inside of me.

So let us confess our sins to God and accept Jesus Christ into our hearts, so He can live in and through our lives by

His Spirit. How do we do this? It is baptism that renews us from the inside out. When we are under the water we are in the grave with Christ, and when we come up from the water, we rise from the dead with Christ. So it is Christ in me who is righteousness, justice, and light. His Spirit is in me and will be in others when people accept Him in their hearts.

CHAPTER 6

CHRIST IS OUR PEACE

P eople wish for world peace. To have world peace, we have to have peace within ourselves. Christ is our peace, and if we accept Christ in our hearts, we will be at peace. Christ is the Prince of Peace, which passes all understanding. God created us with a searching heart for Him. We were born into sin, because of the fall of Adam. We search everywhere for peace in the world. However, Christ brings peace into our hearts. That is why God sent Christ to pay for our sins. People search worldly things to bring them peace, but they are corruptible. Only God who came down to earth to bring incorruptible peace can satisfy our hearts. Christ is our missing piece that brings peace into our hearts.

People try to find peace in this world. They search high and low, but they do not look up to Christ where our peace, redemption, forgiveness, and salvation reside.

Other so-called religions hide sin and mislead people. But the Word of God reveals sin to us. God gives us a choice to repent because Jesus Christ died for you and me. Other so-called religions are the opinions of men. But, as it says in 2 Timothy 3:16-17:

> All Scripture is given by inspiration of God, and is profitable for doctrine, for reproof, for correction, for instruction in righteousness, that the man of God may be complete, thoroughly equipped for every good work.

Also, in 1Timothy 1:8-10, it says:

> But we know that the law is good if one uses it lawfully, knowing this: that the law is not made for a righteous person, but for the lawless and insubordinate, for the ungodly and for sinners, for the unholy and profane, for murderers of fathers and murderers of mothers, for man slayers, for fornicators, for sodomites, for kidnappers, for liars, for perjurers, and if there is any other thing that is contrary to sound doctrine.

The Word of God speaks the truth and doesn't hide anything, but reveals the things that we don't want to talk about. Regardless, as Christ said, the truth will set you free.

In the movie, *The Apostle*, Sonny makes a profound statement that rings true today and that we should all think about: "I would rather die today and go to heaven than live to a hundred and go to hell."

Journal entries:

Saturday, April 20, 2013

I have failed God and I am covered in sin, I make myself sick! And yet the Prince of Peace comes on my behalf and offers His hand to me, and I take it because

He shows me love. His love brings me to my knees and brings repentance. And yet, if I tell my brothers in Christ my sins, some are quick to judge me. I know Christ has taught me that men should not judge each other. Judgment has already come upon Christ when He was on the cross. Yes, there will be a judgment day, but God is the judge, not men. When we sin, Christ shows us love that brings truth into us so that we repent of our sins. Love brings truth while harshness brings evil. When we fall into sin we should bring each other back with love, because it brings the truth out of us all. I love God because He calls me out and corrects me so I can be in His light. I speak to all of us so we may live, love, and repent. Live for Christ, love Christ and his people, while repenting of our sins. My love goes out to you. Please remember God's love is for all.

Thank You, Jesus, for calling me into your light, kingdom, and hanging on the cross for us all.

May 6, Monday, 2013

When I look back on this first year of being a Christian there were a lot of things that I discovered about God and myself. For example, learning how to have faith in Christ even when times are not so good, or how to be led by God. Also how to view God, Christ, and the Holy Spirit as one and realizing they have different roles in our spiritual walk.

Christ has shown me things that were difficult to learn, like how not to doubt. A few months ago I was in a trial for two weeks and it was over me doubting Jesus. But, by the grace of God, I overcame it through His peace that passes all understanding. An additional lesson was how God speaks to my heart and it gives me inner peace within my spirit. I know there are greater challenges than these, but I look forward to them because it's to my benefit as I become stronger for Christ. True, life is hard, but the question is whom do you lean on?

March 3, 2014

These past two weeks I have endured hardship, but thanks to God for He delivered me out of a fiery trial. As I was going through this trial, God revealed to me I needed to acknowledge Him, for I was being prideful. My trust was in myself and not in Christ. In those two weeks of testing God's peace was the anchor in my heart, soul, and mind.

During the trial I prayed without ceasing and was always giving thanks to God, and recollecting what He has done for me. As long as I call on the Lord Christ Jesus, His peace is upon me. To those who want peace let them call on the Lord Christ Jesus:

> Be anxious for nothing, but in everything by prayer
> and supplication, with thanksgiving, let your requests
> be made known to God; and the peace of God, which
> surpasses all understanding, will guard your hearts
> and minds through Christ Jesus.
>
> (Phil. 4:6-7)

Even if we are in hell and high water the peace of Christ will not leave us; for His blood is upon us and separates us from this evil and perverse generation. Let us all acknowledge God and praise Him because it is He who has delivered humanity from our sinful nature. It is Christ's peace that dwells in us when we go through the valley of the shadow of death. He is anchored in all of us; even in those who do not believe, for God created them in His own image.

I knew that every trial I went through would not last forever, even when I felt like I was being swallowed up by my thoughts. I knew I would persevere through it by leaning on God and surrendering myself to Him, for that is how we get Christ's peace. We all need to learn how to surrender to God, not only when we are new converts but also in our daily walks with Christ Jesus.

For if we suffer in this life for bearing the gospel of Christ, at least we know the Prince of Peace will carry us in His bosom in the good times and in our trials. I will acknowledge Christ Jesus always because He is my Savior and humanity's as well. Thanks be to God for showing His love, mercy, grace, and peace through Christ Jesus. May we all strive with our crosses toward Christ Jesus, those who believe and those who soon will be a part of the family of God as well.

CHAPTER 7

BEING STRONG FOR CHRIST

People say they want to be strong for Christ, but they don't know how to be. When we are saved and converted to Christ we trade our weakness for His strength. Our weakness makes us stronger, because we are partakers of Christ's glory. His strength is His love for us.

> Love suffers long and is kind; love does not envy; love does not parade itself, is not puffed up; does not behave rudely, does not seek it's own, is not provoked, thinks no evil; does not rejoice in iniquity, but rejoices in the truth; bears all things, believes all things hopes all things, endures all things. Love never fails. But whether there are prophecies, they will fail; whether there are tongues, they will cease; whether there is knowledge, it will vanish away.
>
> (1 Cor. 13:4-8)

> And now abide faith, hope, love, these three; but the greatest of these is love.
>
> (1 Cor. 13:13)

We can endure all things for Christ has overcome the world. As Christ said to Paul in 2 Corinthians 12:9-10:

> "My grace is sufficient for you, for My strength is made perfect in weakness." Therefore most gladly I will rather boast in my infirmities, that the power of Christ may rest upon me. Therefore I take pleasure in infirmities, in reproaches, in needs, in persecutions, in distresses, for Christ's sake. For when I am weak, then I am strong.

So it is good to suffer and be weak. For Christ went through the same when He hung on the cross, which makes us partakers of His kingdom. So be glad that our King is with us always, even to the ends of the earth.

Journal Entries:

Saturday, March 30, 2013

I have a friend and his name is Jessie, he is a Christian, and also a man who loves Christ and His people. One person who Jessie reminds me of is Job. He was a man in the Old Testament who lost everything but still had faith in God. Jessie has overcome a lot in his life and I respect him because I know he loves God so much and he feeds God's people.

Jessie has helped my mom and me out by securing a used car and fixing it for free. I know Christ was working in my life through Jessie. I love him because he and I and all Christians will be united with Christ. I will always pray for Jessie for he is my brother in Christ. He suffers for others as Christ calls us to do, and that demonstrates his reliance and strength through Christ.

Thank You, Jesus, for calling Jessie and me together. I know You will be here for us in the good times and bad times. I love You Jesus!

Tuesday, April 9th, 2013

We all go through trials, regardless of our backgrounds. Whether we are rich, poor, Christians or non-Christians, we have our difficult times. As Christians we go through trials because Christ suffered for humanity and we are all partakers of Christ and His suffering, which includes His glory as well. Those who have not received salvation don't know how to deal with trials, which is sad. I love them and want to teach them about Christ.

When Christians go through trials we pray, preach to ourselves, read the Word, and most importantly, we have faith in Christ. Even though the circumstances are not what we want, it is the Father's will. Christ is the glory and we the partakers of Him. We are His children and He knew us before the beginning of time.

I speak to the people who are soon to be Christians and who are lost or confused in life right now. Come to Christ and give your heart to Him. Yes, it is a hard road and there are hardships, trials, and tribulations. But with every trial, hardship, and tribulation, there is a glory that allows us to see the Son rise. Remember this my brothers and sisters, for I love you all; and our love comes from Him who loved us first.

Thank You, Jesus, for calling me into your kingdom. For I know that am dead in sin but You renewed me from the inside out. Yes, I sin, but I repent of my sins to You and your blood cleanses me.

Thursday, April 11, 2013

God gave my friend Ray some advice through me about his National Day of Prayer speech in Fort Collins, Colorado. However, something is hindering me and I can't put my finger on it. Nevertheless, with that being said, I know I have to maintain my ways before Christ and stay the course with His strength.

One concern that hinders me is when I hear people take the Lord's name in vain. When people say it, it sticks in my head and I think of saying it. Or it comes across my mind when I am mad or I am impatient about something. Look at me, what a weak man I am! Even though I am dead in sin my heart searches for God's peace in His Word, and I continue to follow Him. If I sin every second of the day, I will repent of my sin every second of the day. I know what I am to this world, which is nothing, but I am something to Christ. I may be weak in my own efforts as a follower of Christ, but He is my strength and that makes me capable to follow Him. I walk through the valley of the shadow of death. I like what the actor, Will Smith, said, "Danger is real, but fear is a choice." I do not fear men, demons, or devils, not even Satan. My fear is in God, not man.

Help me, Lord, for You know I am weak in every sense of the word. Nonetheless, pick me up and clean me, please.

Sunday, April 14, 2013

The Christian life is hard to live. We have doubts, struggles, and hardships. God has created the human body to overcome some things, but the human spirit overcomes everything with God. We are children of God. Yes, we sin, but if we come back to Christ, He shows us love that reveals truth and not harshness and doesn't bring evil.

Tuesday, April 16, 2013

Yesterday a bombing happened in Boston, and my friend, Kyle Sullivan, died in a car crash. I didn't know him that well, but I called Kyle a friend because God calls us friends even though we sin. It was a day of mourning, but with that being said, let us call on the name of Jesus Christ. People call on God when bad things happen to them or others they know. However, we should call on God all the time, for He calls us all the time.

We never know when we will die; only God knows when death is around the corner. We should not be afraid because we are Christians. To the unbeliever, death is the end, but to the believer death is the beginning. Let's be honest, people are afraid of death. Christ said in John 14:6, "I am the way, the truth, and the life." People of the world live until death, but people not of this world live for Christ unto eternity.

I love all of you. Whether you like it or not, Christ knows and loves us all. For Christ gives you His love of truth and life. The world brings harshness that brings evil and death. God bless you; know He is not against you.

April 27, 2013, Friday

Trials? They never get old in the Christian life. Yes, trials are painful and scary in the moment. I have become accustomed to the pain, and I am not scared anymore of trials; peace always follows. One verse out of the book of Job is so powerful and explains my point. Job 13:15: "Though He slay me, yet I will trust in Him. I will maintain my ways before Him." This verse gives me strength because the Christian walk is in the valleys, in the places of the unknown. But God knows the valleys that we will walk through.

You may ask your self how God knows the valleys. Jesus was tested in every way by the Devil and overcame it all; He was already through the valleys. So when we are tested it is for a purpose, to strengthen our faith, reverence, godly fear, and love. When testing comes we should maintain our ways before the Lord as Job said it. The sooner we maintain our ways, the sooner the trial will be over, and we will experience His peace. It is Christ who lives in us; and all of our ways should be always in Him.

Thank You, Lord, for giving me life in your kingdom. You are my true Father. I love You, and say hi to all the saints for me.

September 12, 2013, Thursday

The Christian life is full of tests but in those hard times we have a tendency to drift off and God has to reroute us back to Him. Even though I am tested as I write this journal, I know it is for the glory of God so Christ can shine through our storms. There are three examples that God gave to me about how He shines through our weakness. The examples are Christ's disciples: Thomas, Peter, and Judas Iscariot.

Thomas doubted Christ when He rose from the dead. Peter denied Him three times after Christ told Peter he would deny Him before the event happened. Finally, Judas sold out Christ for thirty pieces of silver to His betrayers so the Scriptures could be fulfilled. Christ told all His disciples that one would betray Him and he knew it was Judas.

We as humans and Christians fall into the old line: "I would never doubt or deny or even sell out Jesus!" The answer is, yes, you will. When testing comes, we as Christians doubt if Christ is real, or with us or not. Even when people say the Lord's name in vain sometimes we as Christians will not speak up about how it is disrespectful towards Him and us. Or when Christians go out to the bars and get drunk or do something they should not be doing, that is like selling out Christ for the world as Judas did.

We have the tendency to doubt God when things don't go our way or when we are tested. Thomas, one of the twelve disciples, doubted that Christ rose from the dead when the others said they saw Him.

> Now Thomas, called the Twin, one of the twelve, was not with them when Jesus came. The other disciples therefore said to him, "We have seen the Lord." So he said to them, "Unless I see in His hands the print of the nails, and put my finger into the print of the nails, and put my hand into His side, I will not believe."
>
> (John 20:24-25)

Christ showed Thomas that He wasn't some earthly man, but rather the heavenly Man.

> And after eight days His disciples were again inside, and Thomas with them. Jesus came, the doors being shut, and stood in the midst, and said, "Peace to you!" Then He said to Thomas, "Reach your finger here, and look at My hands; and reach your hand here, and put it into My side. Do not be unbelieving, but believing." And Thomas answered and said to Him, "My Lord and my God!" Jesus said to him, "Thomas, because you have seen Me, you have believed. Blessed are those who have not seen and yet have believed."
>
> (John 20:26-29)

Peter denied Jesus and Judas betrayed Him. The most interested thing is that Jesus told the two of them what would happen before it happened! Jesus told his disciples:

> Then Jesus said to them, "All of you will be made to stumble because of Me this night, for it is written: 'I will strike the Shepherd, and the sheep of the flock will be scattered. 'But after I have been raised, I will go before you to Galilee."
>
> (Matt. 26:31-32)

This is what Peter said to Jesus:

> Peter answered and said to Him, "Even if all are made to stumble because of You, I will never be made to stumble." Jesus said to him, "Assuredly, I say to you that this night, before the rooster crows, you will deny Me three times."
>
> (Matt. 26:33-34)

It was the same with Judas. Jesus said this to all His disciples at the last supper:

> Now as they were eating, He said, "Assuredly, I say to you, one of you will betray Me." And they were exceedingly sorrowful, and each of them began to say to Him, "Lord, is it I?" He answered and said, "He who dipped his hand with Me in the dish will betray Me. The Son of Man indeed goes just as it is written of Him, but woe to that man by whom the Son of Man is betrayed! It would have been good for that man if he had not been born." Then Judas,

who was betraying Him, answered and said, "Rabbi,
is it I?" He said to him, "You have said it."

(Matt. 26:21-25)

In all of these failures of man, Jesus showed mercy to
them and will to us. Although Judas killed himself, I
know Christ would have forgiven him. Jesus showed
mercy to Thomas and Peter in the gospel of John,
chapters 20 and 21. We must know that Jesus is both
God and man. I know He is God because He points out
man's sins are within in him:

> What comes out of a man, that defiles a man. For
> from within, out of the heart of men, proceed evil
> thoughts, adulteries, fornications, murders, thefts,
> covetousness, wickedness, deceit, lewdness, an evil
> eye, blasphemy, pride, foolishness. All these evil
> things come from within and defile a man.
>
> (Mark 7:20-23)

This shows Jesus is God, because if He isn't, He would
just be like all the rest of the men.

> And without controversy great is the mystery of
> godliness: God was manifested in the flesh, justified
> in the Spirit, seen by angels, preached among the
> Gentiles, believed on in the world, received up in
> glory.
>
> (1 Tim. 3:16)

Even though our thoughts betray us in the world,
our hearts are renewed by the Spirit of God. Does
Mohammed or Buddha challenge humanity more then

Christ did? I think not. For these two men were so-called prophets, but Jesus forgave sin and no prophet ever did that. We are just men, but Jesus is God. He lowered Himself to become a man to give us an example to follow, and so He could die for our sins. And so we, being the weak Christians that we are, could follow Him. Even in our weakest hours we are strong in Him, for He is our strength.

You are my strength and life. Strengthen me as You always have, Lord. See me through the days of my life until You, oh Lord, call me home to be with You.

CHAPTER 8

IDOLIZING

Heathen or pagan idols, have no place in our lives. The world has a lot of them. It's funny because when we say "idols" we think of a golden, silver, or clay image shaped into either an animal or a human being. But, idols can be anything whether they are famous people, sex, money, sports, drugs, music, pets, alcohol, cars, video game consoles, computers, even foreign so-called gods, and the list goes on.

We are in era of time when idols are heavily pressed into our lives and tend to dictate what people do with their lives. God has created us to have faith and to worship Him with our spirit, not with our eyes. The world worships with their sight by putting unreal faith into objects. God asks us to have faith in Him: "For we walk by faith, not by sight" (2 Cor. 5:7). For Christ Jesus is the faceless man. Even the Shroud of Turin is made an idol. God did not make His face known to us. He did not want us to make an idol of His image. God wants us to worship Him and Him only. For it is written, "that no flesh should glory in His presence" (1 Cor. 1:29).

In the book of Genesis we see when God called Abraham his response was by faith, not by his sight. By faith is how we should all lean toward God. But the people of this age want a sign that there is a God who exists. The sign that God has given us is Christ Jesus on the cross. Through His crucifixion and resurrection He reconciled humanity to God the Father:

> He has delivered us from the power of darkness and conveyed us into the kingdom of the Son of His love, in whom we have redemption through His blood, the forgiveness of sins. He is the image of the invisible God, the firstborn over all creation.
> (Col. 1:13-15)

Christ Jesus is the face of the Father who came in the likeness of man to show us what God is like; for Christ did not testify of Himself but of the Father. These idols that people worship so earnestly cannot save them, speak, or hear them. And if this generation has faith in these reckless things that they see, then their faith is dead. But if we put our faith in God, His Spirit shall carry us to the end and into the kingdom of God. "For we through the Spirit eagerly wait for the hope of righteousness by faith" (Gal. 5:5).

I may not have these worldly possessions and make idols out of them, but what I do have is God's Word, which is sound and firm in my life. God's Word may be hard to understand at times. However, I know if I ask Him about specifics in His Word He will bring peace and understanding in His own time.

The people of this age have a void in their hearts; that is why they create new images in vain. Trying to get their heart's desires out of their vanity, they discover how wretched their hearts, souls, and minds are without Christ Jesus. My heart is burdened with these idols in our lives. Do we not understand that anything that is not from God comes from the Devil to entice and seduce us away from Christ Jesus? My generation is just like the Israelites of the old, as it is written:

> Saying to a tree, "You are my father," and to a stone, "You gave birth to me." For they have turned their back to Me, and not their face. But in the time of their trouble they will say, "Arise and save us." But where are your gods that you have made for yourselves? Let them arise, if they can save you in the time of your trouble; for according to the number of your cities are your gods, O Judah.
>
> (Jer. 2:27-28)

I would rather look like a fool in man's eyes, than in God's eyes. We should serve Christ Jesus rather than men. Christians should not idolize themselves because it could lead us to spending more time on ourselves instead of God. In the past I would spend idle time alone thinking of the *what if* questions about God, prophecy, and His Word. God revealed to me that if we spend our time sharing the gospel of Christ with people, all of our fears or *what if* thoughts will vanish. Easier said than done, right? I am confident that if we serve Christ and do not waste our idle time with doubt, we will grow in our relationship and fellowship with God. All of our focus should be on Christ Jesus and the Word of God, so we can teach, share, love, and proclaim Jesus to the underserved.

> Preach the word! Be ready in season and out of season. Convince, rebuke, exhort, with all long suffering and teaching.
>
> (2 Tim. 4:2)

So let the Word of God pierce our hearts, souls, and minds, for we are all bond servants to God through Christ Jesus. Let us not idolize ourselves, men, angels, animals, objects, or anything else, but rather love, worship, trust, serve, hope, and have faith in God through Christ Jesus.

For my love, hope, faith, and trust are in You, Jesus. You have answered my prayers and delivered me from trials and tribulations. I shall always acknowledge you for helping me. I am your child and you are my Father who I love with all my heart, soul, mind, and strength. May your Spirit, light, and power be upon me forever more.

I also pray for those who believe that You may show them the things they need to know and want to know about You and your Word. And for those who are soon to believe in You, I pray they may repent and confess their sins while declaring that You, the Lord Jesus Christ, are their Savior who died for all of us, and was resurrected for our sakes.

I love You Jesus. May I never leave you nor forsake You. Help me to become a man after Your own heart; through You and only You I pray. Amen and amen.

CHAPTER 9

LOOKING FOR EVERY OPPORTUNITY

In one of my journal entries on April 26, 2013, I wrote how it is important to take note of the value of finding every opportunity to witness to people, whether they are Christians or not. Sometimes it's just good practice. At the same time, it can encourage other Christians or plant a seed in someone's life who has never heard about the gospel. I'm reminded of what Paul wrote in Galatians 6:10 (NLT):

> Therefore, whenever we have the opportunity, we should do good to everyone—especially to those in the family of faith.

Also in Ephesians 5:16 (NLT): "Make the most of every opportunity in these evil days."

Let me tell you about three people I ministered to. The first person was my grandmother who led me to the Lord. She is the sweetest woman I know and I thank Christ for bringing her into my life. The second person was Bill, a person I have known for a year and who lives at the same complex as my grandmother. I gave him my business card and I mentioned to Bill that my love and God's love are always for him. Bill started to cry and hugged me and I told him, "I'll keep you in my prayers and you do the same." The third and last person I ministered to was a man named Antonio who works at the Safeway in Old Town; he is a good man. I gave him a business card as well. He hugged me and I told him, "I'll keep you in my prayers and you do the same." The point is that I was led by the Spirit of God to do this and it was so wonderful to see the response. I loved every minute of it.

On Sunday, October 6, 2013, I wrote about my experience of taking the opportunity to witness. I realize this can leave you with awkward feelings, but I know it is for Christ. I talk to many people about Jesus, some at work and outside of work. Some listen and others do not "give a rip" about what I say.

My point is that I can ask people anything about the world and they give me very good answers. And when the tables are turned around and I ask them about Jesus, the wisdom of the world becomes unwise and the might of the world becomes weak. The Scripture says:

Therefore, behold, I will again do a marvelous work among this people, a marvelous work and a wonder; for the wisdom of their wise men shall perish, and the understanding of their prudent men shall be hidden.

(Isa. 29:14)

I can talk to anyone about anything, but when I talk about Christ Jesus I am condemned, looked down upon, considered uneducated, and stupid according to their standards. However, the people who despise me, or anyone else who rests in Christ Jesus, don't do it just to me, but they are despising the One who sent us.

The scripture is clear about this when it says:

"Behold, I lay in Zion a chief corner stone, elect, precious, and he who believes on Him will by no means be put to shame." Therefore, to you who believe, He is precious; but to those who are disobedient, "The stone which the builders rejected has become the chief cornerstone, " and "A stone of stumbling and a rock of offense." They stumble, being disobedient to the word, to which they also were appointed.

(1 Pet. 2:6-8)

Isn't it interesting that people can talk about sex, sports, money, etc. and deny themselves for other people for these worldly things? Yet, when it comes to Jesus Christ, people are frightened to deny themselves for Him and are unwilling to become slaves of righteousness. The apostle Paul said:

I speak in human terms because of the weakness of your flesh. For just as you presented your members as slaves of uncleanness, and of lawlessness leading to more lawlessness, so now present your members as slaves of righteousness for holiness.

(Rom. 6:19)

But we all can see that when Jesus is brought up in various conversations, people are on their toes, because He is not what they want. Even other *so-called Christians* feel uncomfortable talking about Him. But, let me say that all of us need Jesus. I say to you what Christ said to His disciples when two of them asked to sit on His right and left side.

> But Jesus said to them, "You do not know what you ask. Are you able to drink the cup that I drink, and be baptized with the baptism that I am baptized with?"
>
> (Mark 10:38)

He was asking, are you willing to suffer with Christ? That may mean physically, mentally, and spiritually. We as Christians may have to suffer for Christ's name, but it is for the glory of God. We should keep looking for every opportunity to share the love of Jesus. "Many are the afflictions of the righteous, but the Lord delivers him out of them all" (Ps. 34:19).

When it comes down to it, I'll never stop testifying about Jesus Christ who is our Lord. May the Word of God comfort our hearts. God bless all of us who rest in Him, and in Him alone.

Being a Christian is not only just attending church and reading God's Word, but also witnessing to others about Christ Jesus and applying the Word of God in our everyday lives. I have come across many people from all walks of life and shared the gospel of Christ with them.

One evening I saw a man sitting on a bench near the bike path I was riding on. As I rode past him, God compelled me to stop and go back to talk with him. As I was drawing near him I prayed that God would help me speak to this man about Christ. When I came up to him, I saw that he was crying. I asked, "Are you alright?"

"No, I lost my wife in July."

He said his name is Johnny and I introduced myself to him as well. While we were talking, I shared with him how I lost my step brother Sage, who was killed by a car flying off the road while he was walking home in the bicycle lane. I expressed how I could relate to his loss. I asked him, "Are you a Christian?"

"Yes, I am," he responded. "And I meet with a pastor once a week to help me study the Bible." He told me that he had to leave soon and I asked him if I could pray for him, which I did. As we parted ways I kept praying for Johnny because I felt his pain. I was happy to answer God's call and to meet Johnny's needs as well.

The point of my story is that as Christians it is our duty to look for every opportunity to share and serve Christ whether people are Christians or not.

Another example is when I came across four people on the Poudre River bike trail while I was riding my bike to my mom's work. The first man I encountered was Steve. I saw him from a distance and prayed that God would help me share the gospel with him. I came beside him and started to talk with him. He shared how beautiful the outdoors was, which led to him talking about how a house trailer fell on him and broke his pelvis. From that he had to have a hip replacement. The doctors told Steve he wouldn't walk again, yet, it was obvious he was walking. After introducing ourselves, I said to him, "Did you have faith in God while you were going through your injury incident?"

He answered, "Yes, I made peace with God while I was under that trailer, and I made my peace with God while I was in the military service too." Steve seemed very happy while I was talking to him. I could tell he loved nature because toward the end of our walk, we stopped and he said, "I do not know how atheists say there is no God when we have all this in front of us."

I agreed with him and said, "Everything has a purpose."

"Yes, even the minuscule things," he said.

"Yes, even the dirt has a purpose," I added.

Steve then again told me he had reached a place in his life where he made peace with God. He said, "I believe that God is not dead, but I don't believe in organized religion."

"What would you identify yourself as?"

"If I had to pick something, I'd be a Mormon, but I wouldn't be a good Mormon," Steve said.

Steve's response was a perfect example of how people are confused about God. We have so many Christian denominations that people do not know who the real Jesus is anymore. Some of this is due to pride and arrogance and not reading God's Word for themselves. There are false teachers who do not teach from the Bible, nor instruct the people what God commands us to do, and how we are saved through Christ Jesus.

But, at least Steve knows Jesus. At the end of the day all that matters is God's Word and not men's opinions. After my conversation with Steve, I asked him if I could pray for him and he said, "Sure." After praying we said good-bye to each other and parted ways. I told Steve I would keep him in my prayers.

Another man I crossed paths with was Louie. He was sitting on a bench near the Poudre River. As I came near him and sat down on the same bench with him, God led me to talk to him about Christ.

As we were talking about the weather and the river, he asked me my name. Then, "Where are you going to school, Thaylor?"

"I am in a Bible school called Global University, the Berean School of the Bible, to become a pastor. Do you believe in God?" I asked.

"Yes, I do."

We talked about how this world was messed-up and about people who live the fast life and pay for it in the end.

Louie said, "All those drugs and alcohol are no good for you."

"I agree."

Then he asked me, "Do you do that stuff?"

I laughed, saying, "No, I do not do drugs or alcohol. I better not because I am becoming a pastor for Jesus."

Louie said, "You just stay on the long and narrow road; it will be hard but you will be fine." He began to talk to me about his kids and grandkids, and he seemed very happy. But, then he said his wife had died of cancer.

"I'm sorry for your loss."

"She's in a better place now." Then he chuckled and said, "But now I have to take care of her dog." When Louie was about to leave I asked him if I could pray for him and after we prayed we both went our ways.

Soon after I prayed with Louie, I met Ted. Initially, I passed him as I went to see my mom at her work. I returned back to the bridge that overlooks the Poudre River and saw the same man who I passed earlier. I prayed again before I approached Ted and sat next to him in the same place that Louie and I had sat and talked.

"What are you doing?" I asked.

"Just waiting for my ride, trying to enjoy the peaceful moment," he said. For some reason he was irritated about something.

"How's your day going?"

He angrily answered, "I told you I am trying to enjoy a peaceful moment."

"Okay, then I'll leave," I said. While I was leaving I prayed for him. Even though Ted became angry, I realized he was probably going through a hard situation that I did not know about, but God knew what Ted was going through.

People may reject us for trying to share the gospel with them. We servants of God have no reason to judge them, because that is God's job not ours. Sure we may get frustrated with those people but we need to let our frustrations turn into love and peace. All we can do is pray for them. God knows the hearts of all people and He loves them all, even if they hate Him. Our Lord Christ Jesus gave us the two great commandments as the scribes asked Him what is the greatest commandment of all.

> Then one of the scribes came, and having heard them reasoning together, perceiving that He had answered them well, asked Him, "Which is the first commandment of all?" Jesus answered him, "The first of all the commandments is: 'Hear, O Israel, the LORD our God, the LORD is one. And you shall love the LORD your God with all your heart, with all your soul, with all your mind, and with all your strength.' This is the first commandment. And the second, like it, is this: 'You shall love your neighbor as yourself.' There is no other commandment greater than these."
>
> (Mark 12:28-31)

When we as Christians are rejected or treated spitefully by others, let us not take it to heart. For they do not reject us, but they do this to Christ Jesus, who is the Lord and Savior of us all. We are heirs and partakers in His sufferings with Him. When we share and witness the gospel of Christ we represent Christ. Jesus was crucified, not us; and He was raised from the dead, not us. But let us love those who choose to be hateful and spiteful to us for sharing and professing the gospel and pray for them anyway. For as Christ even said:

> But I say to you who hear: Love your enemies, do good to those who hate you, bless those who curse you, and pray for those who spitefully use you.
>
> (Luke 6:27-28)

There was still one more person who I encountered on the same trail and his name is Andrew. Once again, I was compelled by God to talk to this man. I turned around and went toward him, and was praying to God to help me speak to him. While approaching him, I started the conversation by asking about the three white buildings we were walking toward. He answered, "It's the headquarters of the trail."

I introduced myself and we talked more about the history of the buildings. Andrew told me that he was a forest ranger who had moved up here and how he loved nature. He was volunteering for an organization that protects national parks, and he is a substitute teacher for a charter school as well.

"Are you in school?" he asked.

"Yes, I'm studying to be a pastor."

"What denomination?"

"I'm a Christian."

"Oh, so do wear those robes and stuff? Can you get married?"

"No … you might be confusing me with the Catholic practice. Are you a Christian?" I asked.

"No, I am not."

"Can I ask why?"

"I don't believe. But I will say that Jesus was a good teacher. I just love nature a lot." "Do you believe God created everything

...the birds, the creeping things, the beasts of the field and the monsters of the sea and that there has to be a Creator?

"Yes, that is true."

Andrew was set in his ways, but he is on the right track for falling in love with nature, for it is God's handiwork. For it is written:

> The day is Yours, the night also is Yours; You have prepared the light and the sun. You have set all the borders of the earth; You have made summer and winter.
>
> (Ps. 74:16-17)

All creation points back to God and soon Andrew will realize this.

As my conversation was ending with Andrew, I asked Andrew, "Can I give you a Bible and pray for you?"

"I don't think I can take the Bible; I'm not ready yet."

"Well, can I still pray for you?"

"Sure, only three people have prayed for me before."

I prayed for him, and after the prayer Andrew thanked me and said, "Your prayer was very sincere."

"Thank you, Andrew. You know before I came to you, I passed you, and I turned around and asked God to let me talk to you about Jesus."

"He seemed surprised and said to me again, "Thank you very much." After our prayer and brief conversation we parted ways.

April, Vicki, and Madeline are three young ladies who are dear to my heart. I have known them for a while and I appreciate them very much. They are Christians and we have ministered to each other. I know God has used me as an instrument to bring to light the teachings of Christ on a personal level with them. I have become a bond servant laboring for them in Christ. In my hard times they have encouraged me to press on for Christ. Their love for Him is evident. I pray they will grow as strong women of God and minister the gospel of Christ Jesus to others. Amen.

Alex is another dear friend and brother to me. He has known me before I was a Christian and when I first gave my life to Christ. Alex has stood beside me and supported my faith in Christ. He was raised Catholic in his youth, and even though he does not go to church, I know he has a form of godliness within him. Anytime I witness to Alex, I pray to God to show me how to minister to him. Alex and I have had many theological discussions and I have enjoyed all of them.

Once Alex asked me about the apostle John for a school project. Of course I answered his question and told him that John was one of the twelve disciples who was close to Jesus. He wrote one of the gospels, 1, 2 and 3 John, and of course, Revelation. I also told Alex that in John's gospel he refers to himself as "the beloved" or the disciple "whom Jesus loved."

The next week we were talking about Scripture when Alex asked, "How do you know that what John saw in his vision was real? I do not doubt God at all; I just do not trust men because the Bible has been translated some many times ...what if they forgot certain words?"

Alex was referring to the book of Revelation, which was written by John, the last apostle, as he was on the island of Patmos, exiled there by the Romans. As John was in the Spirit, the risen Christ appeared to him and showed him the wonders that would take place. I told Alex, "The Word of God is inspired and God spoke and breathed His words into the prophets and apostles to proclaim the message that was spoken to them by God."

Alex said, "Let's say I tell a person who speaks both Spanish and English to ask another person who only speaks Spanish for a favor of some sort. Don't you think there would be some words lost in translation? I am not trying question you or harass you, I just want to know."

"Yes, I see your point, I said, "but your message did not change. Even though there are different kinds of Bible translations it is to simplify the Word of God for all of us. Even though certain words may be changed, the message has always stayed the same. I have to have faith in God because I know God's Word is true."

Alex responded, "That is a strong faith."

Scripture brings to light the questions that Alex proposed. The apostle Peter speaks to his audience by saying he was and is an eye witness of the sufferings of Christ. He writes:

> And so we have the prophetic word confirmed, which you do well to heed as a light that shines in a dark place, until the day dawns and the morning star rises in your hearts; knowing this first, that no prophecy of Scripture is of any private interpretation, for prophecy never came by the will of man, but holy men of God spoke as they were moved by the Holy Spirit.
>
> (2 Pet. 1:19-21)

Paul assured the young pastor Timothy of the Scriptures and the power behind them, saying:

All Scripture is given by inspiration of God, and is profitable for doctrine, for reproof, for correction, for instruction in righteousness, that the man of God may be complete, thoroughly equipped for every good work.

(2 Tim. 3:16-17)

Most importantly, the Word of God is not an ordinary book. It is not written in man's wisdom, but it is written by the Spirit of God, who brings forth power and might to our hearts, souls, and minds. For the Scripture is true, as it is written:

For the word of God is living and powerful, and sharper than any two-edged sword, piercing even to the division of soul and spirit, and of joints and marrow, and is a discerner of the thoughts and intents of the heart.

(Heb. 4:12)

Some may ask, why *are* there so many different translations of the Bible? Throughout generations, the language and terminology have changed, so the translations are to make the Bible easier to understand, not to hinder us. Our dictionaries have gone through different editions; they add new words and definitions of words due to changing terminology and meanings of words. New editions simplify and modernize our language for us. Any dictionary that is older than five years is out of date, and has to be kept up to date on vocabulary changes.

For every new Bible translation there is a correlation to the original Bible text. According to Dr. Paul Maier, professor at Western Michigan University, the bible was written over a 1500-yet period from approximately 1400 BC to AD 100. It was written in three *key* languages, Hebrew, Aramaic, and Greek. These languages are complex and they have been simplified into our common languages today. Scribes, who were a member of a learned class in ancient Israel through New Testament times, studied the Scriptures and served as copyists, editors, teachers, and jurists. They took the original copy of the Scriptures and copied not just word for word but letter for letter. Copies had to be exactly the same as the original. After the scribes were done copying, the pages were checked three to four times by different professionals. When a particular book of the Scriptures was completed, they would count the phrases for accuracy. In the Word of God there are no missing words, but rather true authenticity.

Even Jesus simplified and interpreted the Old Testament scriptures through parables that He taught to the twelve disciples.

Through my discussion with Alex, God showed me he is hungry for God's Word, and I have always looked for opportunities to witness to him. Alex is gracious to me and has allowed me to pray with and for him. I know that Alex is not far away from salvation. We know that Christ is just a prayer away.

I pray for Alex that the Spirit of Christ may enlighten him to see the true grace, mercy, and love of God. Amen.

The last person who I will mention is Nick, a dear friend and brother in Christ. I enjoy his company. He has shown me the love of Christ in my certain distresses and for that God will bless him. I recite scriptures to him and I know he loves to hear the Word of God. We pray and share our burdens with each other and I love his honesty. Little does he know that is a godly characteristic. His love for Christ is evident and I know if I need anything he will help me and encourage me to press on for Christ.

I pray for Nick that he may be a strong, faithful, and steadfast man in Christ Jesus, our Lord and Savior. I also pray that he teaches his family the instructions of Christ Jesus.

The reason why I have mentioned all these people whom I know, and some I do not know, is simply because I look for every opportunity to share Christ with all people. I do not write these things to shame anyone, but rather to encourage you in Christ. Many people today are led by their emotions, trying to find each other, and they are not willing find God. They are seeking after their soulmates, rather than the soul's Creator.

This Christian life that I live, I cannot live on my own, but through Christ. I live this life to Him who is the mediator between God and man. It is the Spirit of God who leads me, not myself.

God taught me an important lesson at the gym one day. During the end of my workout, I anticipated using a specific abdominal machine, but a man behind me wanted to get on the same machine. He asked me, "Can I workout with you?" When he told me I could use another machine while he used the one I was waiting for, I got irritated. While I was working out on the machine, I felt compelled to apologize to this man. I repented to God because I was not acting Christ-like toward him, but rather rude. As the man was working out on the other machine asked God to help me talk to him and apologize. I walked up to him and said, "If I appeared rude, I want to apologize."

The man said, "No, it's okay man; I appreciate that though."

God showed me something very important: we must look for every opportunity not only to share Christ, but also to be Christ-like to all people. This is not just on Sundays but everyday, for we are the church and were present Christ Jesus.

I pray for all for the people whom I know, as well as the people I do not know, for the love of Christ is evident to all of us. Let the Spirit of God pierce all of our hearts, souls, and minds. For the world is your doorstop and everything in it is yours. I pray we may all have fellowship in Your name and share the gospel of Christ Jesus, the Son of the living God. Amen.

Thank you Jesus, for You are my Lord and Savior, my Rod and Staff. You lead me and correct me, so I may walk in Your will. You are always true, loving, and gracious toward me and for that I thank you, Christ. I know I do not deserve these blessings, but it is through Your Son, in whom I rest and am hidden in, that You bless me, God.

Help me to become a man after Your own heart Lord as king David was. For I want to walk in Your Spirit, light and power, and become the man of God that You need me to be. Please Father, I beg you to ground me deep within Your Spirit. Hide me; but may the world see You upon me, and may all the world know I am a servant of the Most High God. Place upon me the full armor of God, with the helmet of salvation, breastplate of righteousness, the belt buckle of truth around my waist, my feet shod with the gospel of peace, with the shield of faith, and the sword of the Spirit, which is the Word of God. May my love, faith, peace, joy, focus, trust, and acknowledgement, reverence, devotion, assurance, and intimacy, be ground and rooted in You, so I may grow more abundantly and bountifully in Your holy and precious name I pray. Amen and amen.

CHAPTER 10

WALKING IN HIS WILL

I have walked with Jesus for two years now, and I'm learning more about Christ Jesus through the Word of God that testifies of Him. For we who walk with the Almighty know His will and are assured of it by God's Word. Unfortunately, we have a nature that leads us to sin and unrighteousness. I am the first to admit sin dwells in me and tries to put me in captivity. Without God I would not have known my sinful nature. I am a prideful, haughty, short-tempered, and wretched man. The list goes on about me, and not just me, but also the whole world. For the scripture is true: "For all have sinned and fall short of the glory of God" (Rom. 3:23).

God's will is for salvation, redemption, reconciliation, and sanctification. He is a just and a righteous God. For if God is not real, then we would have no knowledge of sin and would be like the beasts of the field, not knowing the difference between right and wrong. But now we know, through the law and the commandments of God, that all humanity has sinned against

God. In the midst of His decrees we see His jealousy for us. However, where there is jealousy, there is also love. Christ Jesus dying on the cross, who is the atonement for our sins, established God's love. For it is written:

> But God demonstrates His own love toward us, in that while we were still sinners, Christ died for us.
>
> (Rom. 5:8)

God's will is for all of us to be saved. We were not created in vain. There is a purpose for our lives, and that is to know God on an intimate level through the Son of God. For do we not see that God's creation is evident? Do we not know His creation has a purpose?

> The heavens declare the glory of God; and the firmament shows His handiwork. Day unto day utters speech, and night unto night reveals knowledge.
>
> (Ps. 19:1-2)

Man is inexcusable when he says, "There is no God." O man of perdition, who are you to make such a statement? For God gives us a choice to abide by His will or our own. God's will is for all humanity and brings reconstruction to our lives; and man's will is nothing more than destruction, selfishness, and sinful desires. We who rest in Christ have already tasted, experienced, and know the truth of God's will.

Walking in God's will is not easy; don't let anybody say that it is. Of course, there are difficult times in our walk with Christ. That's to be expected when you walk with God, because we are living a life that is impossible. But with God it is possible. If we think God will give us everything we want in life while we are walking with Him, then the cross of Christ has ceased its effect.

God is not a genie in a bottle. If He blessed us with everything we want, then He would be condoning our sinful behavior and desires; therefore, He would not be a righteous God. But, since God is righteous and just, He blesses us with what we need. The daunting truth is that Christ already knows what we would do if we got everything we wanted. Some people cannot accept God's will because they would rather have a genie than a righteous God.

People, rather than facing opposition and being forsaken by all, would rather be accepted by each other. For example, Martin Luther King Jr. faced great adversity for preaching the gospel of Christ during the Civil Rights Movement. He shared and ministered the gospel in difficult times and showed his audience there is no difference between ethnicities, and that God's love, mercy, and grace are for all of us, no matter what we look like. As you can imagine, there was great opposition against him. But King walked in God's will even to the point where it cost him his life. You see Martin Luther King Jr. was not accepted by all, but rather forsaken by many because he walked in God's will. For even Jesus said:

> Do not think that I came to bring peace on earth. I did not come to bring peace but a sword. For I have come to "set a man against his father, a daughter against her mother, and a daughter-in-law against her mother-in-law"; and "a man's enemies will be those of his own household."
>
> (Matt. 10:34-36)

The sword of which Christ speaks symbolizes that He came to bring a division or a distinction among the people who followed and had faith in Him. The will of God calls us to be different among all people, and to teach them the gospel of Christ.

Teach me to do Your will, For You are my God; Your Spirit is good. Lead me in the land of uprightness.

(Ps. 143:10)

My heart hungers for God's Word, and I will always walk with Christ and abide in His will.

God, instruct me and whisper Your word into my heart, soul, and mind. I have peace, love, assurance, intimacy, trust, faith, hope, purpose, and reverence in Your will. I will always worship You with my lips and heart. I hunger for Your Spirit.

I spread out my hands to You; My soul longs for You like a thirsty land. Selah.

(Ps. 143:6)

I agree with what Johnny Square, the pastor of Iasis Christ Fellowship Church, once said, "Let people put God on trial." This applies to Caiaphas as well, who put Jesus on trial. The Jews prosecuted Christ and found no fault in Him. Once He was on the cross they suddenly knew who He really was. Jesus even loves those who hate, dispute, and fight with Him. As it is written:

I, even I, am He who blots out your transgressions for My own sake; and I will not remember your sins. Put Me in remembrance; let us contend together; state your case, that you may be acquitted.

(Isa. 43:25-26)

The God of us all, who raised our Lord Christ Jesus from the dead, is calling us to be with Him. So let us walk with God into eternal life. Even though there may be trials and tribulations, we shall triumph over them in His name. When we walk with God, He knows us through our faith in Christ Jesus, not our emotions. For there are some who think that God goes by what we feel, or our emotions, rather than us being led by the Spirit of God. God gave us our emotions to express ourselves to Him and to one another in everything that we do in His name. We are not to be led by our human nature, but by His divine nature, which is His Spirit. God is behind our emotions when we rest in Him, because Christ teaches us how to love. For it is written:

> Beloved, let us love one another, for love is of God; and everyone who loves is born of God and knows God. He who does not love does not know God, for God is love. In this the love of God was manifested toward us, that God has sent His only begotten Son into the world, that we might live through Him. In this is love, not that we loved God, but that He loved us and sent His Son to be the propitiation for our sins. Beloved, if God so loved us, we also ought to love one another.
>
> (1 John 4:7-11)

> You shall love the Lord your God with all your heart, with all your soul, and with all your mind. And the second is like it: You shall love your neighbor as yourself.
>
> (Matt. 22:37, 39)

For if we abide by God's will, He will show us how to love Him as He commanded us to do.

For Christ is risen from the dead. To those who don't believe Jesus was raised from the dead, I ask, if Christ is not risen, where is your pity? But, knowing Christ is risen you have hatred in your hearts. This fulfills the Word of God.

Behold, you despisers, marvel and perish! For I work a work in your days, a work which you will by no means believe, though one were to declare it to you.

(Acts 13:41)

We who rest in Christ Jesus our Lord and Savior shall suffer greatly for His name, but let us remember it is not in vain. I love all of you because God loved you first. The love I have for all of you is His love that is in me. My prayer is that I may see all of you, so we may have fellowship together in the name of our Lord Christ Jesus, who alone is the King of kings and Lord of lords and the Savior of us all.

For you are the Mighty One who sits on Mount Zion and watches over all of us, the One who hears my prayers in my weakness. You, Lord, lead me in Your ways and in Your will. May Your Spirit, light, and power, and the full armor of God, be upon me forevermore. I love You Jesus. Help me become a man after Your own heart. Help me be steadfast in the faith and to share your gospel with all men. Forgive me of my sins, God. I pray that my faith, trust, love, hope, reverence, devotion, assurance, acknowledgment, and intimacy will always be in You and will grow daily. I pray in the name of our Lord and Savior Jesus Christ. Amen and amen.

Journal entries:

May 4, 2013, Saturday

Good-byes are always hard in relationships and friendships. It's even harder when they don't understand the calling that the Lord has called us to do. There are two reasons that may be why there is a lack of understanding: they are not of the faith; or they are of the faith and they put their *wants* before their needs.

If our relationships or friendships end it's always for a reason. The Lord knows what's best for us even when we don't fully agree. We are all called to a higher calling, whether you are a believer or not. One way or another we will meet the Lord. When God calls us to a new chapter in our lives and we have to leave friends or family, it's not the end, but it is a "see ya soon"! The reason why I am writing this is because I have had to depart from friends or family more than once. I would be lying if I said it did not hurt to depart from some friends. But here is the thing, God knows and looks out for our best interests. That is why we need to listen to God's will and not our own. The Lord's will is for everyone and our will is for ourselves. Nevertheless, God still personalizes his directions for us. In Ephesians 5:17(KJV) we read, "Wherefore be ye not unwise, but understanding what the will of the Lord is."

May 29, 2013, Wednesday

People who are not of the faith can suck the spiritual energy out of you if you're not careful. When a new person comes into our lives we may be attracted to them and want to get acquainted with them because our curiosity gets the best of us. When we are fond of a person who isn't of the faith and they get into our personal lives, we as Christians can be in trouble and lose our connection and the leading of the Spirit of God. Sometimes we are led from the path that God has for us.

The reason why I am writing this is because it happened to me. I tried to minister to this person (a girl), and she wasn't prepared to give up her life for Christ. Of course, I was leading myself away from the path that God bestowed on me by putting her first because I liked her. I thought I could lead her to Christ. In reality I was trying to lead myself, instead of God leading me. Slowly but surely I was growing weak and placing Christ on the back-burner, which means I wasn't spending personal time in the Word, causing my relationship with Christ to wane. My heart was convicted to leave my relationship with her because I was being steered away from God. With tears, I asked God to take me away from her because I wanted that peace that I had with Christ before I got involved with this girl. God answered me and I was faithful to my calling to Him, and for that I will always be faithful to my Lord. The point is not to waste time on people who will not listen to the Word of God. Be their friend, of course, but do not let them get between you and God. Walk in the path that God has given you.

June 9, 2013, Sunday

I am always angered when I see people who once knew the true meaning of God's will, and have left Christ for the lusts of the world. People leave Christ for many reasons, such as: money, drugs, alcohol, and other doctrines that claim there are other ways to find God. The verse that comes to mind is:

> The Spirit clearly says that in later times some will abandon the faith and follow deceiving spirits and things taught by demons. Such teachings come through hypocritical liars, whose consciences have been seared as with a hot iron.
>
> (1 Tim. 4:1-2 NIV)

It is sad that people leave for the pleasures of the world that lead to sin and death. Some people who are not believers recognize those who have left the faith and follow them. As Christians we should always remember that hard times come and go. Endure them and you will grow in the faith. Know that people are always watching us, and most importantly God is watching, but He is also showing us His will.

> Here is a trustworthy saying: if we died with him, we will also live with him; if we endure, we will also reign with him. If we disown him, he will also disown us; if we are faithless, he will remain faithful, for he cannot disown himself.
>
> (2 Tim. 2:11-13 NIV)

The key message is to know that we are called to deny ourselves and to follow Christ.

This verse teaches us how to continue our walk in Him:

> If anyone would come after me, he must deny himself and take up his cross daily and follow me.
>
> (Luke 9:23 NIV)

In these times it appears impossible for people to obey this scripture, because the world has become the anchor that holds people down and leads them astray.

People may say they are Christians and act as if they were, but the reality is they put on a mask of godliness while denying the wonders of God. It's interesting because they try to bring the world into the church, when in fact we should bring the church into world. This is a wonderful verse that is powerful and speaks the truth:

> There will be terrible times in the last days. People will be lovers of themselves, lovers of money, boastful, proud, abusive, disobedient to their parents, ungrateful, unholy, without love, unforgiving, slanderous, without self-control, brutal, not lovers of the good, treacherous, rash, conceited, lovers of pleasure rather than lovers of God— having a form of godliness but denying its power. Have nothing to do with them.
>
> (2 Tim. 3:1-5 NIV)

Many people believe that the end is coming soon. As God's children, we need to be ready for Him. We are not that far from Christ. The importance is to know that our sin holds us back from His grace. We all need to come to terms with our spiritual destiny. That's why repentance is crucial when we first come to God. Our repentance is not a one-time occurrence, but it is a lifestyle. Here are some scriptures that speak to this:

> That if you confess with your mouth, "Jesus is Lord," and believe in your heart that God raised him

from the dead, you will be saved. For it is with your heart that you believe and are justified, and it is with your mouth that you confess and are saved. As the Scripture says, "Anyone who trusts in him will never be put to shame." For there is no difference between Jew and Gentile—the same Lord is Lord of all and richly blesses all who call on him, for "Everyone who calls on the name of the Lord will be saved."

(Rom. 10:9-13 NIV)

If we confess our sins, he is faithful and just and will forgive us our sins and purify us from all unrighteousness.

(1 John 1:9 NIV)

My dear children, I write this to you so that you will not sin. But if anybody does sin, we have one who speaks to the Father in our defense—Jesus Christ, the Righteous One.

(1 John 2:1 NIV)

All Scripture is God-breathed and is useful for teaching, rebuking, correcting and training in righteousness, so that the man of God may be thoroughly equipped for every good work.

(2 Tim. 3:16-17 NIV)

The Word of God speaks to these very important topics because God cares about us. The reason why I write my journal comes from God's inspiration. I end with this: God is our Father and we are His children, so let us come to our true and heavenly Father and live the Christian life—that is truly the will of God.

June 24, 2013, Monday

Occasionally, I find it hard to hangout with people who are not of the faith. There is always that void or empty space that is full of nothing. When I hangout with unbelievers I enter their lifestyle, which seems enjoyable at first; then God taps my heart and says, *Don't forget Me.* Once he speaks to me, I snap back into reality and I have to get my bearings back with God.

For example: I was at the pool with a few friends and everything was good; kids were playing and I was having fun. I'll be honest, my attention wasn't on God and then a thought came to my mind, *This will not last forever.* Immediately, I knew I had to get my attitude back with Christ. In this life when the world says it is true, it is too good to be true. Here are two verses that speak reality:

> Jesus answered, "I am the way and the truth and the life. No one comes to the Father except through me."
> (John 14:6 NIV)

Also some of you may say to me, "How can you believe this?" But, it's as Christ told Thomas, the one who doubted that Christ rose from the dead,

> Because you have seen me, you have believed; blessed are those who have not seen and yet have believed.
> (John 20:29 NIV)

June 30, 2013, Sunday

This *so-called* Christianity in America is torturing my spirit, soul, and mind. Deep down, I am incensed by these wolves in sheep's clothing. What I mean is people have a form of godliness on the outside but deny its power on the inside, as it says in 2 Timothy 3:1-5. This is the image of people working for sin and not the Lord. As the Word says:

> For even when we were with you, we gave you this rule: "If a man will not work, he shall not eat."
>
> (2 Thess. 3:10 NIV)

The parallel in Matthew teaches us to work toward learning the Word of God.

> Then He said to His disciples, "The harvest is plentiful but the workers are few."
>
> (Matt. 9:37 NIV)

The harvest is the people, unbelievers, who don't know Christ. The workers are the believers who do the Lord's work not for themselves, but for Christ. The truth of God is in His Word that testifies about Christ Jesus. The Christian life calls us to suffer because Christ suffered.

> It is better, if it is God's will, to suffer for doing good than for doing evil. For Christ died for sins once for all, the righteous for the unrighteous, to bring you to God. He was put to death in the body but made alive by the Spirit.
>
> (1 Pet. 3:17-18 NIV)

> However, if you suffer as a Christian, do not be ashamed, but praise God that you bear that name.
>
> (1 Pet. 4:16 NIV)

People can't comprehend sin because they live in it.
People can't understand God because they lack the
conviction of sin.

CHAPTER 11

SPIRITUAL
LEADERSHIP

S piritual leadership is helping others move from their worldly lifestyles to where God may want them to be or serve. We must be sensitive to the Holy Spirit as our guide in order to lead others. The Holy Spirit holds us accountable and gives each one of us direction as to what to say and when to speak at the right moment.

Journal entries:

May 11, 2013, Saturday

This past week I was at campus gathering, a church youth group for college students. On this particular night, the youth pastor was not there and a young lady, who was considered a worship leader, was teaching about encouragement, which is a good topic. She referenced Revelation 3:16, "So then because thou art lukewarm, and neither cold nor hot, I will spue thee out of my mouth" (KJV).

This scripture talks about the seven churches; Ephesus, Smyrna, Pergamos, Thyatira, Sardis, Philadelphia, and Laodicea. These seven churches allowed sin to creep into the church, which is disruptive to church leadership. That is why Christ said he would vomit them out of his mouth; they were not on fire for Christ.

To me this is not encouragement. The scripture was taken out of context. It's important to read all the chapters for clearer understanding of what the writer was saying. In my opinion, true encouragement is when someone reassures people when they are in their highs and lows in life.

What a great encouragement and example of leadership when God inspired people to write the Bible. Paul is a great example of leadership. He was inspired to write half of the New Testament; he leads by example because he was taught by God's inspiration. Some of his life was in a prison cell, but by the grace of God, Paul encouraged the churches he wrote to in the good and hard times in his life. He also taught them leadership from behind the walls of prison.

The truth of the matter is God wants us on fire for Him out of obedience. As followers of Christ, it is important for us to not allow the world in the church but to have the church in the world. Being lukewarm is being *half-hearted*, or lacking conviction. We all need conviction in our lives to keep us on the path that God has set before us.

My encouragement for you is that we all would fight the good fight of faith. Hardship, trials, heart brokenness, and tribulations come and go. Nevertheless, true leadership through Christ sees its way through these hard times. We do stray off the path, and yes, we do sin, but the key is to repent and get back on track. That's the first step of spiritual leadership.

July 13, 2013, Sunday

I was watching on my laptop a pastor being interviewed who was talking about God and how He is and always will be wonderful. One of the statements he made was, "Pastors who preach about sin are struggling with sin themselves." Let me say this, that whether you are a pastor or not, if we are Christians, it is a fact that we all will struggle with sin. This pastor preaches about grace, but I also believe that salvation is grace as well.

The preaching of the word that God has given me is salvation, suffering, and steadfastness. I call them the "three esses." Now we all know about salvation, how Christ died for our sins and rose from the dead on the third day. And if we repent of our sins and confess that Jesus Christ is our Lord and Savior, we shall be saved.

Suffering is a key thing in the Christian life as it brings strength to one's spirit.

Therefore, since Christ suffered in his body, arm yourselves also with the same attitude, because he who has suffered in the body is done with sin. As a result, he does not live the rest of his earthly life for evil human desires, but rather for the will of God.

(1 Pet. 4:1-2 NIV)

To this you were called, because Christ suffered for you, leaving you an example, that you should follow in his steps.

(1 Pet. 2:21 NIV)

We shall suffer for Christ, as He has suffered for humanity. As children of God we shall imitate the Father. This verse is a perfect one for me to imitate.

For even the Son of Man did not come to be served, but to serve, and to give his life as a ransom for many.
(Mark 10:45 NIV)

Some of you may ask, why is suffering so important in the Christian life? Suffering strengthens us. The Spirit of God is the One who encourages us in hard times.

But the Counselor, the Holy Spirit, whom the Father will send in my name, will teach you all things and will remind you of everything I have said to you.
(John 14:26 NIV)

And if we do suffer let us count it as joy.

However, if you suffer as a Christian, do not be ashamed, but praise God that you bear that name.
(1 Pet. 4:16 NIV)

Let's touch on His steadfastness. Now this means to maintain our relationship with Christ when times get rough in our faith. These verses came to me and fit perfectly in this journal:

> Therefore, since we have been justified through faith, we have peace with God through our Lord Jesus Christ, through whom we have gained access by faith into this grace in which we now stand. And we rejoice in the hope of the glory of God. Not only so, but we also rejoice in our sufferings, because we know that suffering produces perseverance; perseverance, character; and character, hope.
>
> (Rom. 5:1-4 NIV)

If we go through the hardships that await us in life and rely on Christ for strength, our character and faith will be shaped and molded by the hands of God.

> And as for you, brothers, never tire of doing what is good.
>
> (2 Thess. 3:13 NIV)

Leadership requires sacrifice and we will suffer for the cause. I love all of you. If anyone of you suffers, then I myself suffer as well. May we all live for God and not ourselves.

God, You are my strength and I give all the glory to You. It is You who blessed this journal, not I. Father, I love you. Forgive me of my sins!

CHAPTER 12

IT'S NOT JUST ONE WORD OF GOD

In this chapter I will share my thoughts on how to interpret the Bible. However, before I go any further, please know that I am not a professor, nor am I an expert on hermeneutics; but I am currently taking Bible college courses in this field.

We must learn how to interpret the Bible in order to apply it to our lives, hence I want to shed some light on this topic. If we do not learn how to understand the Bible correctly, we fall into the misinterpretation of scriptures for our own benefit, thus generating our own set of rules and regulations that focus on one specific doctrine in the Bible. In some cases, we create doctrine, rather than accepting the whole Word of God. The apostle warns us there is only one gospel:

> But even if we, or an angel from heaven, preach any other gospel to you than what we have preached to you, let him be accursed. As we have said before, so now I say again, if

anyone preaches any other gospel to you than what you have received, let him be accursed.

(Gal.1:8-9)

Scripture equips us to share and live out our faith in Christ. There is only one lawgiver and those who do not live by the law, die by the law. I am torn up and deeply distressed at how some individuals misinterpret Scripture and tend to have their own philosophical thinking that is not biblical, relying on their own opinions rather than God's Spirit and Word.

The Bible is filled with doctrines, which means "teachings." God's Word teaches us about God himself, creation, sin, the law and commandments, baptism, the Holy Spirit, etc., but ultimately about the Son of God who is the cornerstone of the Bible. For it is written:

> All Scripture is given by inspiration of God, and is profitable for doctrine, for reproof, for correction, for instruction in righteousness, that the man of God may be complete, thoroughly equipped for every good work.
>
> (2 Tim. 3:16-17)

If we focus on our opinions and use Scripture to lean our way, then we have misused God's word for personal gain. As a Christian, I urge and encourage you, those who rest in Christ, to discipline and challenge yourselves to be well versed in the Bible, not for my sake, but for everyone's. We should not only read, but also study the Bible and notice the constant themes that God stresses to us about Himself.

I remember when I was witnessing to Frank, a self-proclaimed homosexual, who yet believes in God. He started talking about how we should "put our minds down" and enjoy life. I responded by saying how that was a nice philosophical thought, but I have the mind of Christ. Then I brought up God and said, "Frank, God did not create men to be with each other the same as with women. It is a sinful practice ...and I know we all sin. I don't say this out of my own opinion but I stand for what God stands for."

He said, "Yeah, but I don't feel like I'm sinning though, because God is love and I feel like we are gods. You are prefect, Thaylor, you don't even drink or nothing."

"It is Christ who is perfect in me. And yes I sin everyday and that's why I have to ask forgiveness, for we all have fallen short of the glory of God. And if I say I do not sin, then I make God a liar. Yes, God is love but His love brings conviction. God loves us all but hates our sin." Then I quoted to him the following scriptures:

> For all have sinned and fall short of the glory of God.
>
> (Rom. 3:23)

> If we say that we have not sinned, we make Him a liar, and His word is not in us.
>
> (1 John 1:10 NKJV)

After I quoted these scriptures, Frank did not know how to counter God's word. He only said, "But I feel like God put me and my husband together."

I answered Frank by saying, "That is your own opinion and God gives instructions not opinions."

I know there are Christians who say, "God hates fags." Frank told me, "Yeah, I have heard it all man." I apologized on their behalf and told him that God loves homosexuals but does not approve of their lifestyle and behavior. Even though his opinion may change about me, I explained to Frank that I do not say this on my own authority, but on God's. Frank said, "I can respect that."

I love Frank and his kindness and how he is so open to hearing the gospel. But he interprets "God is love" for his own gain and he does not know what the verse really means. We find this in 1 John: "He who does not love does not know God, for God is love" (1 John 4:8).

The epistle of 1 John is a wonderful letter to read. It's about God and how He is life, light, and love. But we must enter into life, light and love through the Son of God. For the life that God has for us is eternal life, and He is the light, which involves fellowship with Him. That means we confess our sins to God when we have sinned so we may be cleansed by the blood of Christ. In order to understand "God is love" we must interpret the other types of love that are out there to truly understand the love that God has for us.

There are four Greek words that define love with four different meanings: *phileo, storge, eros,* and *agape.* Let's start with phileo, which is an affectionate kind of love, the same love that Christians show each other in a brotherly way, and that is shown throughout the New Testament. Secondly, storge is the kind of family and friendship love, the same love that our parents have for us and we have for them. The third is eros, which is where the word "erotic" comes from. This is a sexual love or attraction that a husband and a wife have for each other. The last, but not least, is agape. This love is unconditional, the same love that God has upon us that sent Christ Jesus to reconcile us to the Father.

So now we see how the love that God has for us is more powerful than the other three. In the Scriptures this godly love is demonstrated perfectly, as it is written:

> But God demonstrates His own love toward us, in that while we were still sinners, Christ died for us.
>
> (Rom. 5:8)

If we say God is love, we acknowledge that we are sinners and God's love is in us all, for the love is Christ who testifies with our spirit. In order to know what the Scriptures mean we must have the Spirit of God and not just carnal thinking. We should adapt to the Word of God. The people of the world use application rather than understanding the interpretation, twisting the message to appease their lifestyles, picking out only what they want to hear, or selecting verses they think are needed. In order to learn and understand the stories and teachings of God, we must apply them to our lives.

There are times when I am taken back by some who lack discipline to read and study the Word. Be an avid reader. For example, let's say that your mother cooked your favorite food for you, but she forgot to add a certain ingredient. You would taste the difference, would you not? Just as we interpret a cookbook and follow every ingredient to know what we are cooking, the same applies to the Bible. In order to understand a verse in a chapter, we must read the whole chapter and book to know what God is saying. The lives that we live are in Christ and not for ourselves. I am glad God has put me in the ministry for this reason: to preach the truth in Christ Jesus.

I write these things to encourage all of you to pray to God for help when you read His word, for it is the spiritual meal for our souls and brings nourishment to the mind and spirit of the body. The Bible is not just a regular book only or a supernatural book only; it is both, a book regularly used to learn about God's supernatural ways. His Word is riddled with fingerprints working through mankind. For if man is the vase, God's Spirit is the flower that never loses its beauty and brings purpose to the vase. So, let us embrace Jesus and His teachings and do what our Lord has commanded us to do. We should allow the Lord to work His will through us.

> And Jesus came and spoke to them, saying, "All authority has been given to Me in heaven and on earth. Go therefore and make disciples of all the nations, baptizing them in the name of the Father and of the Son and of the Holy Spirit, teaching them to observe all things that I have commanded you; and lo, I am with you always, even to the end of the age."
>
> (Matt. 28:18-20)

We must commit ourselves to the Master and follow the doctrine that He lays before us. My commitment is that I will keep myself strong in the gospel and share with all people who Jesus Christ is, and how He taught the apostles to teach us how we should love each other in His name. Let us give our lives to the Lord and God of the universe who watches over us from heaven; the earth is His footstool.

My benediction:

You have blessed me beyond measurement. For who am I to say where is God? You have blessed me with a new day, clothes, food, and shelter. Faithful and True is Your name. I shall not waver in You, for You are my castle who I shout and praise, and say "Who is like the God of Abraham, Isaac, and Jacob?" In my lonely times it was You who visited me in my despair and made me strong again. For when I idolized myself and did not want to speak or think about You, Your word burned within my heart and I was provoked to preach about the prophets of old. Set my heart, soul, and mind on fire for You, Lord. Crush and break my heart for what Your heart breaks for, and lead my tongue in prayer, to ask for what I need and not my wants. Cleanse my spirit from this world with Your Word. Help me fight hate with love and hate unrighteousness that people love. I am Your servant until the end of time and You are my Lord and Savior. Forgive me of my sins; purge these thoughts away from me into the grave were they belong.

I pray Lord that I may be a faithful and true man of God. Help me to love those who hate You, and to share the gospel of Christ to all people. May Your Spirit, light, and power be upon me. And place the full armor of God upon me, including the helmet of salvation, the breastplate of righteousness, the belt buckle of truth wrapped around my waist, my feet shod with the gospel of peace, with the shield of faith, and the sword of the Spirit, which is the Word of God.

I also pray that my faith, love, peace, joy, trust, and focus will be instilled in You forever and ever. I pray for those who I have witnessed to and those who I am going to witness to as well, that they may accept your Word and come to the knowledge that You are the triune God: Father, Son, and Holy Spirit. May we all repent and believe in the Lord Jesus Christ forever and ever. Amen and amen.

CHAPTER 13

MY CONFESSIONS

In these short letters to God, I express to Him how my life or walk is going. By the same token, I confess my sins to God and always ask for forgiveness. In these hard times I give praise to Him for He sees me through these distresses and forgives me as well.

My letters to Christ:

January 16, 2014

Dear Christ Jesus,

I write this letter for I am weak and You are my strength. I give my thanks to You. I don't know how many times You have come to my aid when I am in need. Your Spirit has always ministered to me about who You are and who I am in You. I will worship the King of kings and Lord of lords for You have called me to be Your preacher and to serve those whom you love and care for. I know at times I am tested and tempted, but I always preach to myself, Father. You have taught me that no matter what kind of situation I am in to always minister to myself. And, Father, at times I do want to give up and die or hide in a secret place and never come out.

Father, I have prayed and You have answered me in my distresses for You are my sword and my shield, my rod and my staff. I will never forget what You have delivered me from. May peace, reverence, intimacy, and assurance always follow me until the end of time. Speak and minister to me what I should preach to the people of this world, Father. I give praise and thanksgiving to You, God, for blessing me beyond measurement. I have asked and you have given. For I know I will be a minister for You, Jesus. I pray I will always be strong in you and steadfast in the faith, even when I am weak. Amen!

February 20, 2014

Dear Christ Jesus,

I come to You with my heart and I thank You for always hearing my prayers and for that I give thanks always, my Lord. However, this past week was hard because my mind was being troubled by the enemy. You know I have prayed to You while reading Your Word and holding it while I sleep. Lord, I just pray to You and ask that You please protect me from the enemy. Take me to the mountaintop so I can breathe your fresh air, Father. Lord, I read Your Word and know it very well. I know you will answer my prayers on Your own time. Take away these fearful thoughts that go off and on in my mind; for when I preach Your Word either to myself or to others, my fears all go away. I trust You, Jesus, and love you, and I will not stop pursuing You. The road is hard and rough but You are my rod and staff. I fear You more than anything because You, O God, are my protector and the creator of the universe who knows my ways before I even do them. May my trust, faith, reverence, devotion, assurance, and intimacy always be in You my Father, Lord, Savior, and Protector. Amen.

May 22, 2014

Dear Christ Jesus,

I come to You because I am foolish and my anger is shameful. God, I pray to You; I need Your help to rebuke my anger away from me. When I try to do it on my own, I am helpless. I need Your love to shine within me Father. I hunger for You, God, because it is Your Spirit, light, and power I so desperately need. I may have all the spiritual gifts in the world, but without Your love, God, I am nothing. I do not know the meaning of Your spiritual gifts except through love. It is You, oh God, who is and always will be love. Teach me Your ways Father. My anger is trying to take me over. I hate my flesh and I am ripping myself up from the inside out because I despise it. Father, crush my wildness because I know it is not of You but of me. I cannot put myself in front of You nor can I idolize my anger. Lord Jesus, I pray that You please help me focus on Your Word and to preach Your gospel.

My downfall is my anger and short-temperedness with myself and everyone else. My speech impediment gets worse at times due to my frustrations. The sin that dwells in me is corroding me daily. When I am being impatient or frustrated about something that is pointless, I tend to think of the Lord's name in vain; and that is the same as if I were to say it. I am no better than anyone. Forgive me Father for I am the fool. Please crush and destroy everything that is not of You, my Father.

I need You Jesus more than You need me, and I will always repent of my sins to You. Lead me into your righteousness and in your wise counsel as well. All of my sin and brokenness shows I need You. I shall also seek and embrace You, O God, for you are my strength to my heart, soul, and mind. Father, You and I both know very well that I am not a perfect man and that I fall short everyday; but we both know that when You called me, my conversion was real. I intend to finish the work that You gave me. You are my Lord and Savior. Protect me from the evil in this world, and help me proclaim the gospel of Christ Jesus to all the world. Amen and amen.

July 19, 2014

Dear Lord,

I come to You with praise and thanksgiving even though this week I have been going through some trials. I have thoughts on my mind that I do not wish to discuss on paper but only in prayer to You Father, which I have done and I am still doing. I thank You for listening to my requests. I am distraught in mind, for my greatest fears are in my thoughts. But I know they are only thoughts that are not godly, and are like dust upon my feet.

Lord, help me shake these thoughts from Satan and those who practice all evil. I am Your servant and I will only serve You. Your Spirit is upon me and shows me what is right and wrong. For You are the One who is always with me in the valleys of my life. Strengthen my spirit, soul, and mind. Lord I pray that You sustain me until You come for all of us, those who have been faithful to You. Help me discipline my mind to be in control and not out of control as the beasts of the world. I am brewing with anger when these thoughts come up within me. My inward man says "Stop!" God, You are the Lord of my mind, soul, and spirit; give me the strength to bring every thought into captivity and eradicate it in your name, Father.

Abba, forgive me of my sins, for I know I am a broken man filled with sinful desires that lead to weeping and gnashing of teeth. But I shall endure all these things for

Your name's sake. Nothing can separate me from You Father; no man, demon, devil, or angel, can sever me from You; neither will my thoughts or emotions do the same.

For I have been crucified with Christ and raised from the dead with Him. I shall fear no trial or tribulation. If I go through any distress I know it is for the cross of Christ. I thank you for all You have done for me God, for I know the life I live is for You and also for all the world, to share and proclaim the crucified Christ is risen. Amen and amen.

CONTACT INFORMATION

REDEMPTION
PRESS

To order additional copies of this book, please visit
www.joyinliving.webs.com
Also available on Amazon.com and BarnesandNoble.com
Or by calling toll free 1-844-2REDEEM

CPSIA information can be obtained
at www.ICGtesting.com
Printed in the USA
FSOW01n0824111114
3434FS

9 781632 327840